Revolutionize YOUR RIDING

achieving harmony in movement between horse and rider

SUSAN McBANE

D&C
David and Charles

A DAVID & CHARLES BOOK
Copyright © David & Charles Limited 2007

David & Charles is an F+W Publications Inc. company
4700 East Galbraith Road
Cincinnati, OH 45236

First published in the UK in 2008

Text copyright © Susan McBane 2008

Photographs copyright © Horsepix 2008, Sally and David Waters
except those listed below.
With its roots in horse country and staffed by horse people, Horsepix is a
leading provider of high quality equestrian photography.

Page 9 copyright © Sara Stafford, page 47 (bottom) Matthew Roberts,
copyright © David & Charles Limited and page 110 Bob Atkins, copyright
© David & Charles Limited

Illustrations by Maggie Raynor copyright © David & Charles Limited 2008

A catalogue record for this book is available from the
British Library.

ISBN-13: 978-0-7153-2740-1 hardback
ISBN-10: 0-7153-2740-2 hardback

Printed in China by Shenzhen RR Donnelley Printing Co. Ltd
for David & Charles
Brunel House   Newton Abbot   Devon

Commissioning Editor Jane Trollope
Assistant Editor Emily Rae
Project Editor Jo Weeks
Designer Jodie Lystor and Alistair Barnes
Production Controller Beverley Richardson

Visit our website at www.davidandcharles.co.uk

David & Charles books are available from all good bookshops;
alternatively you can contact our Orderline on 0870 9908222
or write to us at FREEPOST EX2 110, D&C Direct, Newton
Abbot, TQ12 4ZZ (no stamp required UK only); US customers
call 800-289-0963 and Canadian customers call 800-840-5220.

Contents

Introduction

It was probably the title that made you pick up or buy this book. I can assure you that the methods described in this book do revolutionize people's riding if they carry them out properly and I stand by my guarantee, below.

I GUARANTEE...

... if you faithfully follow the steps, instructions and advice in this book and put them into practice, your riding will be changed and improved beyond your belief – assuming that you don't ride this way already, that is.
You will have a closer, more trusting relationship with your horse, who will be calmer, more cooperative and happier to work, or rather play, with you. He will become your partner rather than your vehicle or tool.
Your performance together, whether hacking out or competing at international level, will be safer, better, less stressful, much more rewarding and often truly exhilarating.
It will appear to onlookers, and feel to you and your horse, effortless compared with other common styles of riding.

Here are some comments I have had from people who were new to this method, many of them very experienced riders:
'I feel as though at last I've found what that I've been looking for all my life.'
'Why does my horse just seem to understand what I want, even though he's never been trained this way?'
'I can't believe it. He isn't fighting me any more, he's just doing it.'
'I've read about riding like this and seen it, but I never thought I'd be able to do it myself.'
'That's the first time I've finished a lesson and not felt exhausted.'
'I feel as though we're a pair at last. What a relief!'

and this, my favourite …
'It's like coming home.'

What to expect

This book is almost entirely about you and your riding techniques and attitudes. It is not about schooling your horse or about horse management, although these topics are touched on when necessary. Because of that, I will assume that the horse or horses with which you are practising the principles described are well-behaved and trustworthy, willing and attentive, and reasonably well-schooled in that they normally do what you ask. When you are learning to ride, or learning new techniques, it is helpful, indeed almost essential, to have a horse that you don't have to worry about controlling and one that is not likely to try to get you off or to avoid the issue at every opportunity. If this doesn't seem to be your horse, don't worry – the way of riding described in this book will give him every opportunity to become like this. Some horses are 'difficult' because of their past experiences, some

extremely so, and these are not ideal to learn on. However, applying this system will help them and even transform them, if you give it a fair chance, and allow time for the pair of you to gel. I have seen it have excellent results with many horses and ponies.

It should go without saying that other factors come into the matter. Your horse needs to be free of any physical hindrances to learning: he must not be in discomfort or pain anywhere in his body. His tack must be comfortable. He must feel well. Even if he is fine now, he may have bad memories of discomfort and pain – you will have to allow for these. This will slow down your progress, but progress you will still make. However, use your judgement, it remains a fact that you will learn quicker on a horse with no hang-ups, whether he is your own or someone else's. If the latter, then you can transfer your newfound skills to your own horse later.

It always helps your riding if you and your horse get on together. However, even if you don't, riding well and kindly is bound to improve your relationship

'This book describes — in simple and basic terms that anyone can understand — the essentials of a system of riding that cooperates with the horse's natural way of being, with his body and with his mind. This system works. Please re-read the comments of some of my clients on page four and believe them because they are true.'

One of the reasons people want to improve (or revolutionize) their riding is that their horse does not go as well as they would like. Partly, this depends on his conformation and action but partly on his attitude to being ridden. Riding today gradually, and in general, seems to have become harsher than in previous generations and it is not surprising that many horses do not seem to like being ridden, and object to it either subtly or more obviously. Some poor things just tolerate it unhappily, meanwhile trying to do their best out of sheer generosity. None of these situations is a good or kind way of going on. I will cover some aspects of bad riding and bad attitudes to horses, so that you can see what to avoid – in teachers, trainers and riding companions.

What I ask of you

When we learn anything new, or different from what we are used to, it feels strange to us and we can't do it automatically. Our bodies and our minds have to get used to it. New 'nervous pathways' are actually physically created in us to cope with learning new skills.

Do you remember learning to read and write, learning to ride a bike, to work a computer, to ride a pony, to drive a car, to learn a language, and then another language? All these things felt strange and difficult at first, but if you put your mind to it you probably succeeded at most of them. You will be able to think of lots of other things you have mastered – and you can master the skills for revolutionizing your riding, too, because your body and brain are geared towards learning. If they weren't you would not survive.

Learning a new or different system of riding is very like learning a new language. If you can speak one foreign language and then begin to try to learn another, you won't get far if you constantly fall back into the first one or always compare the new one with it. You have to 'clean the slate', 'clear the decks' and open up your mind to the different words and phrases of your new language. The secret to learning anything new (or a new version of something you know already) is being open-minded. You are never too old to be open-minded because it is all to do with your attitude of mind. That is the only thing which prevents it. If you want to be open-minded you can be. If you don't, you can't.

The system of riding you will learn about in this book may be a new language to you, or a dialect, or even just an accent, of the language you know already, but, from

'The secret to learning anything new is being open-minded.'

my experience as a teacher, most people can't 'speak' it and it always comes as a relief and a revelation to them. If you do open your mind and put into practice the techniques described (the words and phrases of your new language), not letting your other language muddy the waters, you *will* revolutionize your riding. I could go so far as to say that your horse will love you for it but I would be accused of anthropomorphizing if I did. (The reason your horse will love you for it, is that it makes it so much easier for him to do what you ask, easier for both of you in fact.)

Be open-minded

On page eight, you will see the word 'classical'. Please don't stop reading and give up. This book is not a classical riding manual but is meant to (and I think it does) set out a simple, logical method you can follow. There is a lot of misunderstanding about classical riding. It is not all to do with 'fancy stuff' that 'no ordinary rider' could or would want to do. The basics will help anyone – tremendously – who cares about their horse enough to give it a genuine try. It applies to any discipline because it is about how horses move and think. I repeat, IT WORKS.

What I ask of you is that:

• you clear your mind of your previous 'language' so that there are no obstacles to learning the new one

• you give this system a fair trial, not giving up if at first it feels strange (like driving a car or typing, your mind and body will both get used to it if you keep doing it)

• you accept that the system is simple and pro both horse and rider

• you accept that it works – and has done for thousands of horses for hundreds of years.

Note: for simplicity, throughout 'rider' refers to anyone who has a relationship with the horse, such as groom, rider, trainer, owner and so on. Although horses are referred to as 'he', the female of the species is included, and although the rider is often referred to as she, men are not excluded.

Learning something new can expand your horizons and make for magic moments for both of you

How I found this system

I started riding as a child at a small riding school owned by an ex-army instructor, Percy Collins, who used the methods of Weedon (the former British military equestrian academy) and Saumur, which is still thriving, with its famous Cadre Noir, and which teaches the modern, French style of classical riding. The horses and ponies we rode were all traditional schoolmaster animals trained in those principles by Mr Collins. Those too small for him to ride he schooled on long-reins, and the better riders among his small staff and clients rode them at first. Lightness, minimal aids, self-carriage (in horse and rider), rapport with and consideration for your mount, and discipline were the order of the day.

After Mr Collins retired, I could not find a similar riding school so rode sporadically mainly on friends' and acquaintances' horses, and continued to read avidly about riding. I finally managed to buy my own horse when I left college and started work. At this point, I was told that my ideas were obsolete and that nobody rode like that any more. Riding in general seemed to me to have been dumbed down and hardened and, compared with the methods on which I was brought up, most of it felt like using a blunt instrument.

I did not encounter anything similar to Mr Collins' techniques until 1981, when I was approached by Dési Lorent. A French-speaking Belgian, Dési had studied in Portugal over many years with probably the greatest classical rider and trainer of the 20th century, Nuño Oliveira, who had brought the art of lightness in equitation to what must surely be its ultimate form. Dési offered me a weekend's accommodation and tuition if I would write about his establishment and riding system in *Equi*, a magazine I was publishing at the time.

'Dési awoke my curiosity when he said he taught classical riding, "which the English badly need to know about".'

The first 10 minutes or so of my first lesson with Dési were mental torture. By then fairly well indoctrinated in other ways, I could do nothing with my mount, Algor, a beautiful Andalusian stallion and a perfect gentleman. Dési explained the principles and aids of his 'Master's method', as he always described it, and Algor began to understand me. As we were cantering round a corner, I realized with a flash of recognition that I actually knew this language or something rather like it. It was as though a door had opened into the past and I was back home, riding like I did when I was a child.

So it wasn't obsolete after all. I was on cloud nine, Algor was galvanized and Dési accused me of making a fool of him!

I studied with Dési for two years, when I could, learning Oliveira's system and comparing it with other classical methods, including those of my youth. I have had a few other classical teachers since then, but always go back to the way Dési taught because I have never found anything better. It is this system that I explain in this book with compatible additions from other sources, including modern equine science and behaviour.

Just because something is grounded in tradition does not mean that it is writ in stone. Discoveries are made and research is carried out, and these sometimes mean that attitudes and accepted mores need to change. In some cases, reverting to previous practices is the answer to modern deterioration. In others, increased knowledge through research into the horse's body and mind, and how they work, must certainly be incorporated into our riding and horse care practices if we are to progress humanely and effectively.

Self-carriage on the weight of the rein – the ultimate aim in top quality equitation, whatever the discipline

Enable your horse to do what you ask

It may sound like a strange thing to say – 'enable' a horse to do what you are asking – but it isn't really. For most riders the problem is persuading a horse to do a particular thing. It can be so frustrating to give what you truly believe are clear and correct aids for a particular movement or way of going, even something very simple, and to have nothing happen.

Even worse is when the horse reacts in a way you do not want and were not expecting, and worse still is when or if he reacts somewhat violently and you almost lose control, actually lose control or even part company. All these results (or lack of them) are because in some way or another your horse has not been enabled to do as you ask.

You and your horse need to be best friends ...

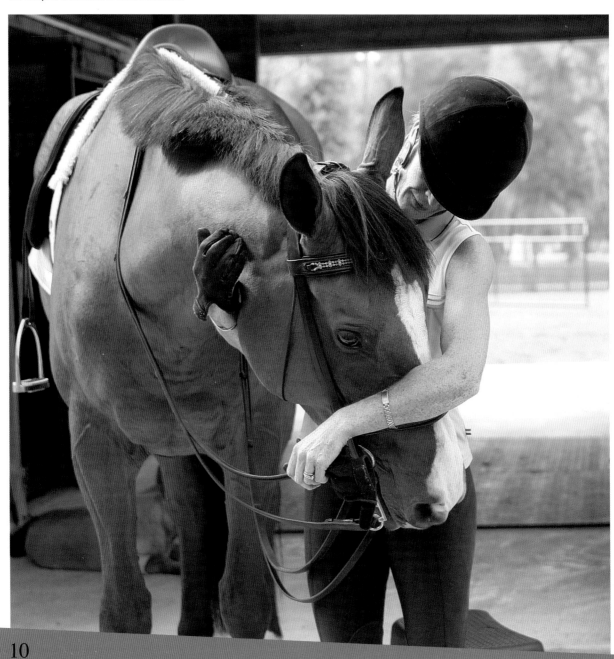

... but horses also need the chance to make and be with their equine friends, too

What is going wrong?

Not all horses are cooperative by nature, but in my experience most of them are, most of the time – unless they have an excellent reason not to be. The reason will not be merely because they don't feel like doing it (most will go along with it even then) but more likely because:

· *they don't understand* what the rider means
· *they are mentally distracted*, inattentive, confused, upset, excited or angry – all emotions that greatly interfere with a horse's willingness and ability to concentrate on what his rider is asking for. This is common in horses that haven't bonded with their rider
· *they are physically incapable* of doing what has been asked due to conformational problems, physical weakness and/or lack of

fitness, an injury their rider has not spotted and which causes pain, or due to a lack of natural athletic ability
· *they are afraid* of attempting it because they expect it to cause them discomfort or pain or it is too difficult for them, like a big jump or complex dressage movement
· *they are tired*, mentally, physically or both. This often happens during schooling sessions, which should be kept short – 20 to 40 minutes is plenty with very frequent breaks on a loose rein
· *the rider is preventing them from cooperating*, albeit unintentionally by creating tension (which worries many horses) or giving conflicting aids so that they don't know which to obey

Of course, a few horses are lazy or unwilling by nature, and this should also be taken into account.

Bonds and bonding

Horses, as we know, are social animals. Lone horses almost always feel unhappy and insecure. Where equine companionship cannot be supplied, it is often recommended that they are provided with other company, such as being grazed next to cattle, or having a sheep, goat, cat or donkey in their field or stable. These animals may be better than nothing but even the donkey will be a very poor substitute for another horse or pony. (I always feel sorry for stallions when they are kept, as is traditional

but by no means essential, away from other horses. It is no wonder that so many of them have digestive, behavioural and other problems due to distress.)

Where do humans fit in? In order to form a strong and mutually meaningful relationship, horse and rider need to like each other and feel 'right' in each other's company. A horse that lacks a bond with his owner will never be truly relaxed and confident in her company. Even if he is not afraid or nervous, he will be to some degree distracted and aware of the fact that he'd rather be somewhere else, doing something else, with someone else, either a different person or a horse. A horse that is always calling to or looking out for other horses when he is with his rider is showing, clearly, that this person is not his preferred companion and that he is not much interested in what she wants. Because he feels safer with other horses (otherwise he would not be constantly wanting to be with them), this behaviour also reveals that the horse doesn't even feel particularly safe with his owner. Similarly, a person who is to some degree afraid or unsure of her horse – lacking in confidence – will never relax sufficiently for the horse to think, 'She's in charge of our situation. I'm quite safe with her. Everything's OK. Let's go!' To forge this kind of

friendship, you need always to have a positive, happy and caring attitude when you are with your horse because he will most definitely know how you are feeling, and how you feel about him. Good relationships can happen very quickly or they can take time – sometimes a year or more – but when they're in place everything is much easier.

> ### Bonding in brief
> · **Horses need company – equine company if possible.**
> · **A horse needs to trust his owner or rider – he will sense and**
>   **react to fear or lack of confidence.**

Lots of freedom with enjoyable company goes a long way to keeping horses healthy and balanced in body, mind and spirit

The importance of stimulation

Because they evolved as prey animals, needing to be alert to possible danger, horses are not dullards but need mental stimulation and occupation. Although feral horses do not have a wide variety of activities, they are occupied most of the time, unlike many domestic ones. They also have freedom – a priceless commodity – so they can make choices that are informed and educated by their environment and contact with other animals, not only other horses. In domesticity, what we need to do is make being with us so safe, interesting and enjoyable that our horse is interested in – and genuinely wants to try to do – what we are asking. We want a horse that enjoys 'playing games' and performing strange but easy

movements, which can be quite fun. We also want a horse that likes being looked after and fed, of course, but also likes migrating around the territory (hacking out) to see what's going on, and is quite happy to do so with only us for company. In activities where other horses are also involved, even if he is excited, he needs to listen first and foremost to his rider's wishes and requests, not objecting when other horses pass him yet being confident enough to go in front if asked. As a strong friendship develops, a horse will often leave his friends to be with his owner in the field, even though he knows she does not carry food. He feels right with her, safe, content, sure of not being hurt or distressed, and often confident of being entertained. This all makes for calmness and relaxation.

Physical incapability and discomfort

Under saddle, I am sure that many horses are suffering discomfort or pain that their owners do not know about. Sometimes a slight injury may be causing pain but not actual lameness so the owner does not recognize that the horse's 'difficult' behaviour or inhibited way of going is because something hurts. Pain is 'dis-enabling' the horse from doing what you are asking.

Tack and training equipment are key sources of significant discomfort. The current fashions for high bits and tight nosebands, saddles that are too deeply gusseted at the back, which causes undue pressure, and training aids that are adjusted to force the horse into a shape rather than suggesting a beneficial way of going, all cause discomfort and maybe pain, as do saddles that do not fit properly and/or are placed too far forward. These inevitably result in mental distraction, anxiety, psychological and muscular tension and an understandable inclination to dislike or even fear the activity that causes them. It is a natural part of a horse's defence and survival mechanism to avoid discomfort and pain, so these situations also provide excellent reasons for him to be uncooperative or difficult. We are thus creating circumstances that actually prevent our horses cooperating. (See also pp.60–69, for more information on tack and other causes of discomfort.)

This horse is distracted and listening, with his left ear, to something behind him and to the left. The rider also looks a little uncomfortable. Little progress will be made until calmness and concentration are restored

Sky is distracted by some horses playing about in a field out of shot, and objecting to work. Jo will regain his attention tactfully before resuming schooling

'No horse can be relaxed and have a mind open and available to concentrate on his rider if he is unhappy, insecure, agitated or uncomfortable. The rider may get some sort of a response but nothing like that she would get if the horse were comfortable and calm. The horse is also learning that riding, schooling, and all things connected with humans cause pain and discomfort, whereas we want him to learn exactly the opposite.'

Are you preventing your horse from cooperating?

A horse may be calm, comfortable, ready and willing to work or play with you – but you may not be. You may be nervous or even afraid because of past mishaps, such as falling off, riding a spooky horse, riding a horse that goes badly, is hard to ride, is uncomfortable, or one that generally misbehaves under saddle and pays little attention to the rider, maybe even one whose ambition in life seems to be to get his rider off at the earliest opportunity. Even

This horse is subtly resisting being ridden. His facial expression is tense and his tail is swishing, which can indicate irritation and annoyance

This rider could well be thinking 'I'll take this as a "no" then.' The horse, resisting more strongly, clearly objects to whatever she has asked for

if you are not afraid, you may be anxious or waiting for trouble, not looking forward to your ride and, therefore, not in a particularly positive and happy frame of mind.

Any of these feelings will make you more or less tense, and this will transmit to your horse. Unless he is a traditional, old-style schoolmaster whose métier is putting riders at ease (see p.18), he may wonder why you are tense, he will certainly take his cue from you and either start being jumpy, distracted (looking for trouble or a way out of the situation) or simply unsettled. With all this goes impaired learning, poor performance, maybe arguments, lost tempers and a generally frustrating, disappointing time for both of you.

Emotions very definitely affect our bodies. Certain hormones are produced in response to them. For example, feelings such as excitement and fear stimulate adrenaline, which causes the flight or fight response. Another physical response to adverse emotions is actual physical tension and anxiety, which create stiff and tense muscles. All muscles should alternate between contraction (when they shorten and feel hard) and relaxation (when they are lengthened and feel softer). In between these two states is a condition called 'tone', in which the muscles are slightly contracted. This occurs, for example, when you are holding your body in a certain position without much effort or use of energy and certainly without stiffness or rigidity, but you are ready to be active if necessary. Muscles that are significantly tense and contracted much of the time create a pull on their tendons and do not rest adequately. They will hamper your horse's movement, probably making it stiff and hard rather than smooth and flowing, so the quality of his performance will suffer, and he will be reluctant to work with you. In reality, although you do not mean to do so, you are preventing your horse doing what you wish, or at least doing it as well as you wish. What a miserable existence for both of you!

It's about TRUST and relaxation

Some people like their horses to be fired up and a bit on edge, to give a certain sparkle to their performance, but the essence of true, high-class horsemanship is a horse that is relaxed and calm, working confidently, feeling for his rider's aids, listening for her voice and performing not merely with acceptance but also enjoyment. How could any rider be nervous, tense or frustrated on such a horse?

Only a few horses could perform like this under a nervous, tense or frustrated rider. Some purposely seem to try to put their rider at ease but most do not really enjoy their work if they know that their rider is not happy. To do their best, both horse and rider need to trust their partner, and trust can only come from a mutual feeling of comfort, security and safety.

'It's all in the mind – learning to relax your mind will relax your body and relax your horse.'

Although it's important to relax on horseback, don't take the word relaxation too literally. If we were completely relaxed we would fall down in a heap. I use the word to mean lack of anxiety, untoward tension and any other unwanted emotion that is going to interfere with mutual trust and communication.

Throughout this book you will find tips and advice on how to relax your mind and body. For now we will look at how relaxed you are on your horse and how to start improving the calmness of your mind and body.

The start of enjoying or learning anything is to be calm and happy together, like this pair

Where do you begin?

You need to be open-minded and calm, firm and positive. You have to learn to trust your horse, even if he doesn't trust you – yet – and you need to develop your leadership skills and exude confidence.

OPEN YOUR MIND

As I mentioned in the introduction: when you start learning anything you need to have an open mind, one that is receptive to ideas and principles different from those by which you have worked previously. Almost without exception, and understandably, the clients to whom I teach this system start their first lesson riding the way they have ridden before. They soon find that I am looking for something rather different from what they have been taught. When I ask them to do something that they have not done before (such as use a weight or position aid or an outside rein aid to turn, see pp.120–143). I first explain it simply and carefully. Now, some people absorb the instructions and get it beautifully right first time and, therefore, so does their horse. These people are open-minded enough to try something new without also bringing in preconceived ideas or old habits and practices. However, most people do not respond like this. Often, they half do what I have asked and half what they have done before. They may be concerned about doing something their horse is not schooled to respond to (in fact, horses respond naturally to this system) or they may simply feel strange doing something different and new. Remember that anything new or different feels strange at first, not only in riding.

'Humans form habits just as efficiently as horses do, and they can be very hard to break – but they can be broken IF we are open-minded and willing to really put effort into whatever we are trying to do.'

BE CALM, FIRM AND POSITIVE

Many of the riders I come across are not really relaxed on their horses, even on horses they trust. Perhaps they have been taught the outdated concept that they 'have to show the horse who's boss' and start out from the very beginning in a domineering, confrontational manner. Most horses are not naturally confrontational and this attitude can upset them. As mentioned earlier, most want to do things with us but, naturally, they also want to feel safe, secure and happy. They cannot feel like that with an owner who is tense, wary and bossy, particularly if they expect, from past experience, to be coerced into doing something frightening, stressful or even painful.

'Horses respect and respond to a calm, firm, positive attitude and calm, firm, positive handling and riding.'

If you find you are not relaxed, calm down and look at the horse in a different way. He is not your enemy; he wants to be your friend. He may be the kind of horse who needs a measure of leadership or guidance, protection and reassurance or he may be self-contained and confident and not willing to be mistreated. In either case, horses respect and respond to a calm, firm, positive attitude and calm, firm, positive handling and riding. Give your horse the chance and the time to absorb your attitude and get to know you.

Bearing in mind those three qualities (calm, firm, positive), ride from the start with relaxed, controlled seat, legs and mind, and have still hands with a comforting, adaptable contact. You trust your horse so there is no reason to be otherwise. This attitude adjustment can alter your relationship amazingly in just a few minutes. Your horse will feel more confident in you and, for your part, you are enabling him to work well for you.

LEARN TO TRUST

What about the many people who have horses they do not trust? We need to ask why the horses are behaving in such a way as to cause anxiety and tension in their riders. Almost invariably, I find that it is because some person at some time (not necessarily the person who has called me in to help) has made life uncomfortable, painful, distressing, worrying or confusing for them. They now associate being ridden with angst, or worse. Their new rider has problems with them from the start and, not unnaturally, may become tense and wary. Not many riders really relish being put in danger by an animal as quick-thinking, reactive and hefty as a horse. This anxiety, in turn, transmits to the horse and confirms what he already firmly believes – he's in for a tense, uncomfortable and probably distressing time, as usual. He may play up out of self-protection, fear or anger, and this may result in more pain, or he may stoically put up with being ridden in a demanding, inflexible, driving way, and try to understand and do what seems to be wanted.

If this seems to be a description of your horse, again the trick is to alter your attitude. Really work at cultivating the qualities of 'calm, firm and positive' and gradually you will find that the challenge of 'having' to get on a horse you don't trust (unless he is actually dangerous) will dwindle to manageable proportions and, eventually, you will *want* to ride him and you will start to look forward to and enjoy your rides.

CULTIVATE CONFIDENCE AND LEADERSHIP QUALITIES

What about the horse that seems to be weighing you up (which horses do very quickly and usually accurately) and then either tries to take charge or becomes a nervous wreck because he does not perceive you as a 'safe place' to be? These are two results of the horse having formed an opinion of you and they depend on his temperament. If he, or very often she, tries to take charge, you have a strong-minded animal that likes his or her own way. If he becomes nervous and lacking in confidence, you have one that prefers, in human terms, to be a follower but of someone who is strong and represents security.

In either case, the answer is to cultivate confidence and a leadership mentality in yourself. Even kidding yourself into adopting a self-confident attitude can be enough – sort of 'whistle a happy tune' time – but it obviously helps if you hone your skills and become as

Confidence, leadership – and fun

good a rider as you can. Whatever kind of horse you are dealing with, 'good' does not only mean 'effective', in that you get results, but also 'humane', in that you make stringent efforts not to cause your horse discomfort, pain, confusion, frustration or fear. You need to use methods that make horse-sense, so the horse understands them, and which create feelings of security and confidence, so that he accepts them.

I repeat, *horses pick up on your attitude and mood*. The 19th-century classical rider, General Alexis-François L'Hotte, coined the famous phrase 'calm, forward and straight' to embody the three most important aims in

schooling a riding horse. I first heard the 'calm, firm and positive' trilogy, set out as essentials for handling and riding horses, from Diccon Carus, BHSI. Both expressions start with 'calm', you'll notice. Calm does not mean namby-pamby, weak or uncaring. It means quiet, it could mean laid back, it can mean strong in the face of taxing situations, quiet determination, persistent insistence and keeping your head, and not least your temper, when all about you is falling apart. Horses recognize this kind of calm as strength and something that can be trusted. They respond positively to it. That's where they want to be. And that is exactly what you want.

Schoolmasters

There are some horses with an exceptionally calm temperament and/or vast experience of the human race; they have learned that humans are often wrong and not brilliant judges of circumstances and they can cope with this knowledge. These are the good, old-fashioned, traditional schoolmasters. They teach us, rather than the other way round. Unless their treatment or the general situation is unbearable, they keep their temper, remain involved and try their very best to do what they believe is required and in the best way possible. They appear to look after their riders even to the extent of ignoring their instructions when they are inappropriate. Such horses and ponies are increasingly rare and worth their weight in gold.

Sadly, few riding schools today maintain correctly schooled schoolmaster horses. There has grown up the attitude that well-schooled horses are 'too good' for novice riders. How mixed up is that? It has always been the tradition and practice (because it is the

sensible and logical way to proceed) that the experienced horses teach the novice riders and the competent riders teach the young horses. Gradually, the roles are reversed as the novice improves and she is given a horse or horses to school. Eventually, she takes over the schooling of the green horses and the horses she has schooled themselves take over the education of the novice riders.

Of course, all horses need keeping up to standard by good riders and need a break from novice riders, and novice riders will never progress if they are not given experience on well-schooled horses. It is a dangerous, but increasingly common, practice for a novice rider to buy a green horse so that they can 'grow up' or 'learn' together. The result is almost always disastrous and discouraging for both.

Whatever the rider does, within reason, whether she rides poorly ...

... or reasonably well, a true schoolmaster cooperates and continues to do his or her job – that of giving confidence and helping to teach the rider

Coping with anxiety

In 'Are you preventing your horse from cooperating?' (see p.14) I talked about how mental anxiety and apprehension in the rider hamper free, forward, flowing, smooth, exhilarating movement. They have the same effect on the horse. It is a natural part of the flight-or-fight response we all possess. An adrenaline rush prepares our muscles for action by contracting them, a little or a lot (you've heard the expression 'rigid with fear'), and this is all too often translated into tension and stiffness, which are not conducive to efficient muscle use. It takes a lot of mental control to remain cool, calm and collected when you're expecting trouble or danger but, together with accurate, effective riding techniques and 'feel', mental control is the most important thing you can cultivate.

Anxiety and apprehension can also cause fidgeting – misdirected energy and movement – as the body is prepared by adrenaline to flee or fight. This will be accompanied by mental distraction (lack of focus and concentration) from the task or movement you and your horse are trying to achieve. The whole scenario results in unnecessary mental and physical fatigue. What a waste of effort! The end results, of course, are poor performance, an unpleasant atmosphere during the work, possible short fuses and – the mother of all disasters – the destruction of mutual trust. Calmness fizzles away, firmness can become coercion or, in some hands, subtle or not-so-subtle brutality, and positivism melts away like a grey horse in fog. Faced with conditions like this, most horses will be reluctant or unable to cooperate. As prey animals, their instinct for self-preservation comes instantly and irresistibly to the fore. Their brains are hard-wired this way. They cannot help it. They will either do something active about it or retreat into a shell of apathy and work like a zombie. Assuming that you don't have a schoolmaster (see box opposite), what is the best way to go on?

VISUALIZATION

Before you even approach your horse, remember the calm, firm and positive rule. Think whatever thoughts normally make you relaxed and happy, either a precious and happy memory or a figment of your imagination such as floating on your back in a warm sea, walking through a scented meadow or curled up on a soft cloud (no, not playing your harp!). These and similar mental images can all be used to help make you feel relaxed and positive (see also pp.112–119).

DROP YOUR SHOULDERS

Physically, tension often gathers in the neck and shoulders, even though we don't realize it. As you are reading this, drop your shoulders an inch. If you couldn't, congratulations – you were not tensed up anyway. If you could, you'll know to watch this point in future, and to tell yourself to keep your shoulders gently pushed back and down.

We need no words

WATCH YOUR POSTURE

Believe it or not, poor posture in the rider will be reflected in the horse. It also makes it impossible for the rider to retain the correct, balanced and still seat necessary for refined aids and the ability to not interfere.

Good, straight posture. It is noticeable that a person who has good posture on the ground will have good posture on a horse

Poor posture, head sticking forward, slouching and general sloppiness, easily becomes a habit, and transfers to the saddle, adversely affecting riding performance and hampering the horse

DO SOME EXERCISES

Begin with two simple exercises to release tension in your neck and shoulders (see pp.106–109 for some loosening up exercises). Releasing these two areas alone will make you feel more free and supple:

• Shoulders

Lift each arm and carefully push it around in a circle, forwards, upwards, backwards and downwards, about three times. Also, lift your shoulders, roll them around and push them up, back and down. Finish by placing them back and down as a 'default' position for when you are riding, or for your general posture, come to that.

• Neck

Gently let your head drop down towards your chest and then roll it round and round to the left and right, going each way about three times, pushing it gently so that you feel a slight pull on the tissues in your neck. Never force it or create so much pull that it hurts. 'No pain, no gain' is not the right way to think of it! If you are actually hurting yourself you are probably causing yourself slight injury.

Swinging your arms around loosens up your shoulders and the joints and tissues in your arms

Roll your shoulders around, up, back and down to supple them up. Many people are tense in their shoulders, which can affect their whole upper body posture and their ability to relax and balance

Roll your head loosely around both ways, without pushing too hard, to loosen your neck and jaw

THINK GOOD THOUGHTS

Remember how fortunate you are to have your horse or to be able to ride. Go and see him. Do not get busy as soon as you arrive. Just 'be a star' – stand still and just be, twinkling happy thoughts! It works. Don't fidget, don't move your feet or hands unless it's necessary. Stand still or squat down non-threateningly in a corner and let him come to you. Admire him, stroke rather than pat him, and do it low down on his neck and shoulder – this is known to relax horses and lower their heart rate. Talk quietly to him and visualize to him the two of you getting along famously, either going out for a walk together or riding. I am sure that horses communicate to each other in pictures and I know that visualizing things to them does get through.

The start of enjoying or learning anything is to be calm and happy together, like this pair

DON'T FORGET TO BREATHE

Increase your ability to relax and be calm with these two techniques:

• Centering

If you are interested in yoga, meditation, t'ai chi, Pilates or other similar modalities, you will be familiar with the concept of 'grounding' yourself and operating from your 'centre'. Basically, this just means feeling yourself quiet, strong, stable, balanced and in contact with the earth. It has a very steadying, reassuring and calming effect, which is a wonderful way to feel when handling or riding horses. Think of your control centre as being just below your navel inside your body. Get your awareness down there and think from there, move from there, walk from there and, when riding, certainly ride from there as opposed to using and moving your head, your hands and your feet too much. You'll find that it really changes your inner view of yourself. (See also Mind power, pp.112–119.)

• Breathing

Another relaxation technique, familiar to many people, is controlled and deep breathing, an important part of yoga practice. It gives you great self-confidence and a quiet strength to know that you can control your nerves in this way. Some people can actually slow their heart rate just by breathing slowly and deeply. Many people, when trying this, raise their shoulders, breathe shallowly and too quickly, without any mental relaxation at all. They don't take it seriously so don't do it properly and rush through it without really thinking about why they are doing it. The idea is to think only of the air coming into your lungs, slowly and gently, and passing out again. At first, try dropping your shoulders down and back and breathing fully down into your abdomen to a count of five, holding it for three, then breathing out to a count of five. Repeat this about four or five times. When riding, breathing in time with your horse's breathing or gait rhythm also helps calmness and 'togetherness'.

'Things don't happen by magic: you have to try. You need to become your own teacher to some extent because you can't have a teacher with you all the time and it is no good riding well in a lesson if you don't continue with the techniques whenever you ride.'

Good riding techniques are applicable for riding at *any* time. Hacking is enjoyable for most horses and riders, and the better you can ride the safer and more enjoyable it will be

TRY A RELAXING MASSAGE

Giving your horse a useful, enjoyable and beneficial basic massage really is easy! You don't need any special knowledge or skills – all it needs to be is a glorified stroking over.

We all stroke our horses (I hope!) and all you need is a little more concentration and a little more pressure on muscular areas. There is nothing to be frightened of and you can't do him any harm. Think either relaxing or stimulating thoughts depending on whether you want to calm him down or perk him up, and stroke him slowly or briskly accordingly. Correct body brushing is a form of massage, and hand-rubbing and stroking are very similar. If you do one, you can do the other. If you enjoy it you might like to consider training as a massage therapist – there are books and home study courses available to start you off. It's a great way to help your own and other people's horses.

Use firm, smooth strokes and lean your weight into the horse

Cup your hands round the legs and rub upwards towards the heart, ending with a light, downward stroke to smooth the hair

Gently rocking the horse's crest from side to side to create a head-swing loosens up the whole poll, jaw and neck area

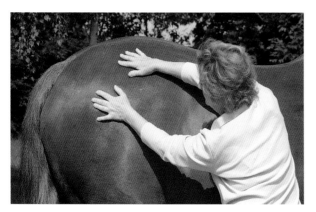

Continue down his body using more pressure on muscular areas

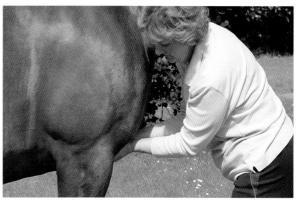

The chest muscles are often overlooked but are much used and will benefit from hand-rubbing or massaging

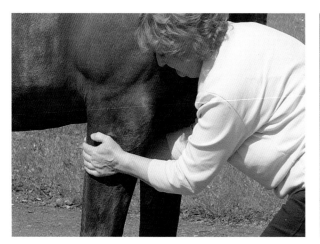

Don't forget the upper leg muscles

Standing with your back to your horse's shoulder and one hand on the far side of his head, gently bring his head around your body to create a passive stretch in which the horse does not need to use his own muscles. Your other hand stays in contact with his body for stability

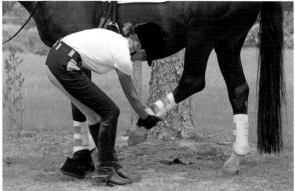

Carefully stretching your horse's legs both forwards and backwards helps loosen him up before work. With the forelegs, make sure you lift them from the knee and then ask for the full stretch. Some practitioners prefer to support the legs by holding one hand under the knee or hock, as well, for safety and the horse's comfort

Coping with a 'situation'

How do you defuse a situation you can feel is about to escalate? For instance, when you are trying unsuccessfully to get your horse to go in a certain way, or perform a certain movement. This is the type of situation in which patience is often lost and nerves get frazzled as you try to succeed. You have an argument and both of you lose confidence in each other. This is the start of fear in the horse and maybe in you, too, and also anger.

• **Stop any pressure, just drop down a gear.** Order yourself to be calm, use one or more of the techniques described on pp.19–25 and make sure that your seat and leg muscles are loose and draped around the horse's back and sides rather than contracted, communicating tension or gripping. If you can school yourself to remain mentally and physically relaxed, your horse will calm down more quickly, particularly if you also stop whatever you were trying to do and diffuse the situation by doing something he does well or enjoys.

• **Do not ride around fuming** because your horse will know how you feel and will remain upset, confused and insecure. If you really cannot keep your temper, get off and lead him and, however hard it is, think pleasant, peaceful thoughts and stroke, don't pat, your horse low on his neck. Bear in mind that when things go wrong it is almost always the human's fault, not the horse's. Consider all the reasons for lack of cooperation (see pp.11–15). It is never worth wrecking your relationship by gritting your teeth and 'riding through' the situation unless you are absolutely certain, beyond a shadow of a doubt, that the horse is simply being obtuse.

• **It is never, ever acceptable for anyone in any circumstances to beat up a horse.** It is even worse to do so to make ourselves feel better. It never teaches a horse anything but to resent his rider and to hate his work. It certainly does not 'punish' him or 'teach him a lesson' or, indeed, 'show him who's boss'. If you need to work out your temper, do it out of sight and earshot of your horse and on something inanimate. Regain your demeanour as soon as possible and return to your horse with loving, bright thoughts and soft conversation to reassure him. If you find containing your temper an ongoing problem, consider going on an anger-management course. Certainly do not ride or handle your horse if you are in a temper because a horse can never know the reasons why, only that you are in a dangerous mood. This puts him on guard and we all know where that can lead.

1

At the time of our photo shoot, Alice and her Irish Sports Horse mare, Brodie, had only been together for two weeks, also Brodie had never visited this manège before and was anxious about the set up and what she was going to be asked to do. Here, she is subtly resisting Alice's gentle rein aid. She is pushing up and outwards against the bit, her back is flat and she is rather tense

Doing something simple that your horse understands is calming and reassuring, so you can resort to it if a 'situation' is developing. Lucy and Anne habitually use some suppling lateral movements during their warm-up and Lucy is well used to this routine

Despite Alice's gentle contact, something has clearly triggered a memory here and Brodie throws up her head in alarm. Dropping the contact like this is exactly the right way to calm and reassure a worried or fractious horse in such circumstances

That good, old-fashioned quality, equestrian tact, reassures Brodie that she can relax with Alice and she drops her head, starts to round up and calm down. Forcing a horse in Brodie's state of mind to accept a firm contact is absolutely not the thing to do

'Self-control and the maintenance of calmness, firmness and a positive attitude come more easily the more you practise them, and they are absolutely essential for learning, progress and a good relationship.'

Is this really training?

Some 'trainers' habitually thrash a horse at the beginning of a lesson or schooling session to warn him not to 'try it on', to show him 'what he'll get' if he doesn't come up to scratch and – that mouldy, old chestnut – 'show him who's boss' from the start. *This is absolute overt brutality* which clearly demonstrates beyond doubt that the person hasn't the foggiest idea of how horses think and learn, that he or she has completely the wrong attitude towards them and is absolutely unsuitable for associating with them in any way, never mind 'training' them. No caring, intelligent owner would want such a person to have anything to do with their horse.

It is common to see horses being worked, tied down – and therefore forced – into a posture where the face is well behind the vertical.

Some people even strap horses into this position and leave them standing in their stables, sometimes for hours at a time. *This is inhumane and a result of wrong thinking and lack of understanding.* Two common 'excuses' for doing it are: it helps the horse to develop the right muscles, and it teaches him to accept the bit and 'makes his mouth'. In fact, it cannot do either of these things, but it can cause pain, stress, strain, physical damage and psychological distress. I am an equine shiatsu therapist, and I have treated several horses that had been abused in this way – all were suffering pain in the head, neck, shoulders and back.

If you are looking for help with your horse's schooling and your own riding, avoid anyone who uses any of these practices, and any similar ones, for the sake of both you and your horse.

How the horse moves

A long way back in our evolution, we were four-legged animals. Horses, of course, are four-legged and, like other similar four-legged animals, have a particular way of getting along that is still ingrained deep in our subconscious from our own four-legged days. If you get down on all fours (hands and knees, not feet because our hind legs are now too long) and walk along like a baby crawling, you will find that you move both limbs on one side first, then the two on the other side, and you will almost certainly start moving with a hind leg – so you might go left knee, left hand, right knee, right hand and so on. Of course, due to our evolutionary development, you will not be able to trot and canter without a lot of difficulty and possibly pain, but you get the message. In evolutionary terms, therefore, you move like your horse and this way of moving is still there in your psyche (see also How you move, pp.70–73).

Conformation

Horses and ponies come in all shapes, sizes, breeds and types. Breeds with studbooks all have a 'type' standard, which can be very hard for 'outsiders' to detect, although it comes with practice. Conformation is a different matter. There are basic rules that most well-proportioned animals fit into roughly. Study the photographs here and the drawings overleaf then look at your horse and, while not exactly comparing him with them, do a bit of measuring up and see what his proportions are. Decide whether or not he has good conformation and what type he is.

The whole subject of conformation and action is really fascinating once you get into it. We don't have the space for a great deal of detail, here, but let's consider a few more noteworthy undesirable points and see what might be the likely effects on your horse's way of going.

'The effects of non-perfect conformation can be slight or very significant on a horse's action and even his soundness. However, a horse may have quite a bad fault, but a good feature elsewhere that compensates for it.'

This pony is a chunky type of good, all-round, family pony, with good, basic well-balanced conformation. He stands squarely with 'a leg at each corner'. He may appear a little long in the body, but has a good long front which gives an overall impression of length in the body. The actual distance between his withers and loins is quite short

Thoroughbred horses and their crosses were born for speed and scope. Their long legs and sleek lines indicate their heritage and abilities. This horse has very open stifles and elbows, indicating scope and a long stride, and his deep barrel (ribcage) suggests plenty of lung room for efficient breathing at high speeds

An attractive skewbald (coloured) mare with an interested outlook. Coloured horses and ponies of various types, from ponies to blood-horse types, are currently very popular and making a name as excellent performers, given good conformation and action

A very attractive native pony type in the primitive dun (buckskin) colouring. He has really good conformation, is neat, balanced and strong-looking. Such ponies usually become children's ponies and although they normally have good temperaments they also have a lot of character

• A horse with a big, heavy head and a long neck will find it hard to be well-balanced overall. He could feel heavy in the hand and 'on the forehand'. He may be prone to tripping and stumbling. If, however, his neck is medium to short, or his head is small, these points will compensate and improve his agility and the way he feels when ridden.

• A horse with an 'upright' shoulder, which often seems to go with upright pasterns, too, will probably give a somewhat jarring ride because the concussion experienced at every step is not absorbed and dissipated. The rider will also feel that she has 'nothing in front of her' but if the neck is fairly long this feeling will be lessened.

• A horse with 'tied-in' elbows, which do not permit the width of three fingers between the point of the elbow and the horse's ribcage will not be able to reach out his foreleg very far and will have shortish strides in front. This makes for a choppy ride in some horses, although I had a horse with this conformation many years ago that was a very comfortable ride. A well laid-back shoulder helps.

• A horse with a very short back, although strong, can have problems with over-reaching where his hind feet continually catch his front pasterns and heels. Sometimes such horses are not very agile and can give a jarring ride if they also have upright shoulders, but this is not always the case. It can be difficult to find a saddle that is short enough for the horse but long enough for the rider.

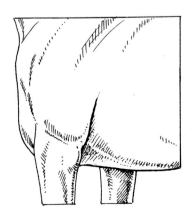

• **A horse with a long back** often seems to lurch along and move the rider a lot. Long backs can also be weak but good conformation in all other important respects can help. Such horses are often not very agile.

• **A horse with short and, usually, weak hindquarters** cannot normally stand up to much work, particularly power work such as jumping and sprinting, as he cannot provide the essential thrust from behind – his 'engine'. If he has good hind leg conformation and is otherwise well conformed and kept reasonably fit, he can perform moderate work well enough.

• **A horse with 'cow hocks'**, that is where the hocks point in towards each other a good deal and where, often, the hind feet correspondingly point outwards, will have weak hind legs and will be prone to stress injuries. However, a very slight tendency towards cow hocks is natural in the horse family.

• **A horse that goes 'close behind'**, that is where you cannot fit the width of a hoof between the two hind feet either when standing or moving, is prone to hitting himself with his hooves and may trip himself up.

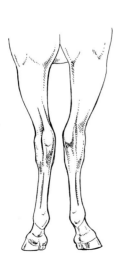

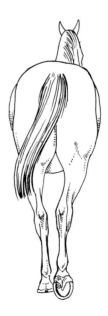

Action

Horses with the action most suitable for athletic work carry their hind legs immediately following their forelegs – no swinging out or in. If you stand immediately in front of a horse trotting towards you, you should barely be aware that he has any hind legs because you will hardly be able to see them. It is the same from the back – the hind legs should follow the forelegs through the same 'airspace'. This action, known as 'true' or 'straight' action, is desirable because such horses rarely hit themselves and don't waste energy moving their feet off a straight track. The force of hitting the ground, and the weight of the rider from above, transfers as evenly as possible up and down the legs with no untoward twisting or uneven stresses caused by crooked action. The more stress the leg is under, the more chance there is of strain and injury.

Not all good performers have dead straight action, but it is something to aim for and is an important point. If you have a horse with 'untrue' action (action which is not straight), your farrier may be able to correct it, at least partially. Many farriers say that it is not possible to alter the action of mature horses. However, in practice this is not entirely true, particularly if the horse is moving badly due to inappropriate trimming and/or shoeing rather than because of his natural conformation. If your horse does not move straight, it is well worth asking your vet and farrier what can be done to help him.

Some breeds of horse, usually of Spanish and Portuguese ancestry, have been deliberately bred to 'dish', which means that they throw their front hooves outwards, particularly in trot, because this is felt by tradition to be extravagant, demonstrative or 'flashy'. This action can be disconcerting to sit on if you are not used to it because it causes the forehand to rock a little from side to side. For most of the requirements of a riding horse today, most people would prefer a horse to have straight action, and some Iberians are now being bred without the dish.

Let's have a look at how the horse moves in the different gaits and when jumping, in a practical way that can be related to how it affects riding.

A lovely elegant and athletic trot that is showing both spring and reach, under a well-balanced rider. The horse is going correctly, with the front of his face *not* behind an imaginary vertical line dropped from his forehead to the ground

'If you stand immediately in front of a horse trotting towards you, you should barely be aware that he has any hind legs because you will hardly be able to see them.'

Dead straight action in trot – just what you want

Dishing, where a horse swings his forelegs out to the sides, is purposely bred for in some breeds as it is felt to look showy. However, in athletic horses it is not usually wanted as it can cause a sideways, rocking ride and is regarded as wasteful of energy

Plaiting is where a horse brings his forefeet directly in front of each other in movement. This type of action can lead to injury as the horse's legs may hit each other, or even trip each other up

Halt

In halt, provided the horse is standing reasonably well-balanced, he will have 'a leg at each corner' like a table, perhaps not so square but approximately so. This is a very stable stance, much more so than our two-legged one. If you have taken your dog for a walk, or led your horse in hand somewhere, on a very windy day, you must have noticed how easily your animal friend keeps his balance despite the elements, while you might be fighting to maintain yours, or even finding it hard to stay on your feet.

Due to a special arrangement of ligaments in his legs, fore and hind, the horse can doze heavily and sleep lightly standing up, even with one hind leg 'cocked', or resting, with the hip down. For a prey animal like a horse, this is very useful as if danger threatens he is already on his feet and can gallop off away from the threat in a very few seconds.

Brodie standing absolutely square and with a good head carriage – in hand and to attention. Alice, her rider, is in an excellent, balanced seat

Moving off

Before a horse moves off from halt, he may adjust the position of his head and neck. He needs to ensure that his hindquarters are light enough to make it easy to lift the hind leg to start off, so if his head and neck happen to be high, perhaps because he is looking at something in the distance, he will often lower them a little to lighten the hindquarters, then move off on a hind leg.

Lucy, an Irish Draught x Thoroughbred with a dash of Shire, adjusts her weight to move off from halt by slightly lifting her head and moving her weight on to her quarters, starting her stride with her left fore. Often, horses bring their weight forward to lighten the hindquarters and start their stride with a hind foot

Walk

When your horse wants to move off into walk from a balanced position, he will almost always move a hind leg first followed by the foreleg on the same side. Then the hind leg on the other side comes forward, followed by the foreleg on that side – and so he progresses, say, left hind, left fore, right hind, right fore, and so on. The horse moves his legs individually in lateral pairs, the two on one side and then the two on the other side, and each foot hits the ground separately, giving four distinct beats to the gait. (A stride, in any gait, is a complete sequence of four footfalls. A step is one foot rising and landing.) There is no time when the horse is 'in suspension', that is up in the air with no feet on the ground. This makes it a very stable gait.

Horses walk by landing one lateral pair of hooves, then the other. Here, the horse has landed his left hind and, just after it, his left fore. His right hind has only just landed and his right fore is lifting to move forward

The left hind is still fully grounded, weight is passing over the left fore, the right hind is fully grounded and the right fore is moving forward

The left hind is about to leave the ground, the left fore and right hind are bearing nearly all the weight and the right fore is still airborne

The left hind has lifted and the left fore and right hind are the sole weight bearers. The right fore is just about to land to complete the sequence of four beats

THE HORSE'S BODY IN WALK

As a hind foot is lifted, the back on that side loses its support and dips down; as it lands and pushes against the ground the back on that side rises again. At the same time, the other hind foot is lifting, then landing, so the back on that side dips and rises similarly. This happens alternately, obviously, in time with the hind feet lifting and landing, and a rider with a relaxed seat and legs can feel the back dipping from one side to the other with each step of a hind foot. For example, say the left hind foot lands and pushes the horse forwards, the relaxed rider will feel an upward and forward push on that side and a dipping on the right side, then a 'lift' on the right side while the left side dips, and so it goes on.

Another effect of this movement is that the horse's ribcage and belly swing from side to side, a bit like a barrel on a rope swinging from side to side, the rope being the horse's spine. As the left hind lifts and the left side of the back dips, the belly swings to the right and a sensitive, relaxed rider will be able to feel this against her right leg. As the left hind lands again and the right one lifts, the belly and ribcage swing left. To revolutionize your riding you need to learn to feel what the hind feet are doing under you and, most importantly, how to use this knowledge to adapt your seat and legs to the horse's movement (see Chapter 5, How to move together, pp.74–105).

In walk the horse's head and neck swing from side to side and back to front. This is more noticeable in

As the horse's right hind lifts and the right hip drops, the barrel swings to the left and pushes against the rider's left leg

When the left hind is in the air (here just landed), the barrel swings to the right and pushes against the rider's right leg

These two photographs show that our hips also dip and rise as our 'hind' legs leave the ground, in just the same way as those of a horse. Following a horse's hip and back movements, therefore, is quite natural as we do it, too

Thoroughbred and Arab horses – or those that contain a good deal of that blood in their breeding – than in ponies, cobs or heavier horses. The head swings to the side of the landing foreleg: if the left foreleg is landing the head will be swinging left and a little down, and vice versa.

The movement of the head and neck is important to the horse and helps him to make effortless strides, which is why it is so vital not to hang onto his head when riding. The head and neck make up his balancing pole and restricting them unreasonably forces him to balance and move using unaccustomed muscles, which is, obviously, much harder work for him. If these muscles are used habitually, they will develop and appear to change his shape and natural action.

The tail is always a dead giveaway as to the quality of the horse's movement. In a correctly moving, relaxed and supple (loose) horse, the tail will swing from the dock from side to side with the movement of the hind legs; as the hind leg and hip on one side move forward, the dock will swing towards that side. If the tail does not swing, you can be sure, injury apart, that the horse is tense. Asking yourself why he is tense can produce some interesting answers! He may be tense because of exciting surroundings or he has seen a friend in the distance. He may also be tense because he is anxious or worried about being ridden or because he is uncomfortable due, perhaps, to badly fitting tack or the rider's technique.

The horse's head and neck are his balancing pole, equivalent to our arms. Alexa gives Ike, a 17-year-old much loved family pony, a loose rein, and as his left fore lands, his head swings the same way

As his right fore lands his head swings right. This is a horse's natural way of balancing his body in walk

A good sign of a relaxed back in a horse is that the dock, a continuation of the spine, swings from side to side. Here, Brodie's right hind is on the ground and her right hip forward; her dock swings to the right

When Brodie's left hind is on the ground, her left hip is forward and her tail swings to the left from the dock

Trot

In trot the horse moves his legs in diagonal pairs. The two legs of each pair move together so there are only two beats to the gait. The left hind and right fore come forward together and hit the ground at the same time. Then the horse springs up off that 'diagonal', as it is known, into the air during a moment of suspension. During this moment, the other diagonal – right hind and left fore – comes forward. He lands on that diagonal and springs up again off it into another moment of suspension, and so on. Due to the horse's being off the ground as much as he is on it, the trot is not quite as stable as walk. The head does not swing in the same way from side to side but the tail certainly does: if it does not, you know that the horse is not properly calm and relaxed. (It would be interesting to note who is riding him at this point.)

Many horses ridden in what has become a very common fashion with a restricted head and neck do not (because they cannot) swing their backs as they should,

and as is natural. Although these horses appear to extend their gaits, it is often an exaggerated and apparently forced extension that is unnatural to and uncomfortable for the horse. If you watch very closely, you will see that their heads, necks and backs are stiff, even rigid, and that they often move mainly from the stifle and elbow rather than from the shoulder and hip with a freer head and neck and a swinging back and tail. Such horses remind me of sideboards on moveable legs.

In trot, the back and hips dip and rise with the hind leg beats, as described for walk, but the rider also has to contend with the significant up-and-down movement of the back as the horse alternates between the moment of suspension during which the spine arches a little, and landing from it when the spine drops a little. Many, many people, at all levels of riding, cannot do a soft sitting trot that absorbs the horse's movement – this is something I address later (in chapter 5, pp.82–87), but please be patient and read on, rather than skipping there now.

'A horse moving naturally in trot, with free, flowing gaits, a comfortable head and neck, a swinging back and a loosely swinging tail is a truly beautiful sight.'

1

Brodie is trotting along freely. She is on her left diagonal (left hind and right fore on the ground), which is about to push her up into the air

2

A split second later, it has done so, and she is in the suspension phase of trot as the right diagonal (right hind, left fore) swings forward

As a horse's hind foot on a given side lifts to come through the air, her hip and back on that side dip as they have lost their support. Here in trot, Lucy's right hind is coming forward and her right hip is dipping

On the other diagonal, as the left hind is in the air, her hip on that side dips likewise. The rider's hips and thighs should be loose and passive so that she can allow her seat to similarly follow her horse's back movements

The right diagonal has landed and the left is coming forward again

Brodie is back in suspension as her right diagonal has pushed her up into the air, and the left diagonal is about to land once more

Canter

In canter, the horse can move with either his right or left foreleg 'leading'. We use the term leading because the horse appears to be pointing or leading the way with a particular foreleg. In fact, the leading leg is the last one in the stride to land. The horse begins a canter stride with the hind leg on the opposite side to the leading foreleg – so if the horse is cantering with the right (fore)leg leading (right canter), the first foot to hit the ground is his left hind. It is followed by his right hind and left fore feet, which land together. Finally, his right fore foot, the 'leading' leg, lands. From this point – after the leading foot lifts and the left hind is coming forward again to land and begin a new stride – there is a moment of suspension.

In a right-lead canter, as the left hind foot comes forward and hits the ground, the rider will feel a slight lift of the forehand. The next beat the rider feels is the right hind and left fore landing together, during which the horse's body levels out horizontally. Finally, the leading (right) foreleg comes forward and hits the ground. As the horse's weight moves forward over it, the hindquarters are felt to lift a little, then the body levels out again in the air during the moment of suspension when all the hooves are gathered up under the horse. The sequence begins again as the left hind comes forward to begin the next stride.

The horse 'bounds' forward from stride to stride in this rocking, three-beat movement. His head and neck naturally and gently undulate slightly with his trunk, up and back as the first hind foot comes to land and down and forward as the leading foreleg lands. As in trot, the spine slightly lifts and dips during, respectively, the moment of suspension and the landing. Again, the swing of the

The canter stride begins with a hind foot on the ground, as the first beat. Here, Ike is starting a left-lead canter stride with his right hind

The second beat shows Ike with his left hind and right fore on the ground ...

tail – and the back if you can spot it – tells an onlooker whether or not the horse is moving in a relaxed, athletic manner or is tense and stiff.

Many riders have problems in achieving canter on the required leading leg and in maintaining canter. This is largely due to not being taught how to sit in accordance with the horse's back movements. If this describes you, see pp.92–94 in chapter 5, but for now, I'd like to help by explaining a feature of the horse's back in canter that is not commonly known. (I learnt it from Dési Lorent, p.8, whose explanation I have used here, and he told me he learnt it from Nuño Oliveira.)

This time let's choose left canter. During most of a left-canter stride, the left side of the horse's back is positioned very slightly in advance of the right side as a result of the left legs moving and landing further forward than the right (see photo sequence below). The left hind lands further forward than the right hind, and the left fore lands further forward than the right fore. During the moment of suspension, when the right hind is coming forward to land again, it moves in front of the left hind creating, shall we say, a 'lateral undulation'. A sensitive rider with loose seat and leg muscles can feel a slight upward movement under their right seat bone in that moment. But it is absolutely momentary. The emphasis, in practical terms, during left canter is on the left side of the back being slightly in front of the right side. The rider must mirror this natural positioning of the horse's back, if she is to be in harmony with the movement – in right canter, the horse's right side is slightly forward and the rider should mirror this, too. (More on this later, pp.92–94.)

... and the third beat shows his left fore on the ground, about to lift into the suspension phase

Here, Ike's right hind is just landing from suspension to start another stride

'In left-lead canter, during most of the canter stride, the left side of the horse's back is positioned very slightly in advance of the right side as a result of the left legs moving and landing further forward than the right.'

Gallop

In gallop, the sequence of footfalls is more strung out, as it were but, of course, the horse still goes with one or the other foreleg leading. To gallop with the right fore leading, the left hind lands followed by the right hind, then the left fore and finally the right fore. This creates a rapid four-beat rhythm with one moment of suspension after the leading leg lands and when the spine is arched upwards a little.

In the gallop, the head and neck movements are much more exaggerated than in the canter, and the spine also moves up and down more. Full engagement of the hindquarters, to bring the hind feet well forward under the belly, is created by the flexing of the lumbo-sacral joint at the croup. The part of the spine behind the croup and in front of the tail is called the sacrum and consists of five vertebrae fused together into a virtually solid plate of bone.

The gallop stride with the right fore leading begins, as with right canter, with the left hind hitting the ground

The right hind then hits the ground and, unlike the canter, there is a pause before ...

Specialist runners

Some four-legged, predatory, specialist running animals like cheetahs and greyhounds have two moments of suspension – the one the horse does not have being in the middle of the sequence after the second hind foot lands and the spine is dipping downwards, so the body is stretched out to its full extent. Along with their much more flexible spine which enables the hind feet to come right to the front, even in front, of the body, this produces a much longer stride, giving these mammals their extreme speed. Having said that, the galloping speed of horses and dogs is about the same.

... the horse flies through the air in the suspension phase before, shown here, the left hind makes contact with the ground again to start another stride. Throughout this sequence, note the swing of the head up and back and down and forward, and the natural position of the head at an angle of about 45 degrees. These two features enable the horse to balance and stride effectively and to breathe at maximum capacity with an unrestricted throat area and, therefore, windpipe

The lumbo-sacral joint is the joint between the sacrum and the last lumbar (loin) vertebra.

The horse tilts his pelvis under him (which opens or flexes the lumbo-sacral joint) when he wants to 'sit' on his quarters, which he needs to do in some advanced ridden movements, when stopping a vehicle at speed with the breeching strap behind his thighs or when doing a sudden stop in the field or under saddle. Tilting his pelvis brings his hind legs under him, because they are joined to the pelvis at the hip joints. This is what is meant by 'engagement of the quarters', although the actual movement is generated by muscles under the spine in this area and attached to the thigh bones.

3

4

... the left fore hits the ground. This 'spreads out' the stride so that the horse can cover more ground

The right (leading) fore then contacts the ground and ...

5

Jumping

When jumping the horse approaches and balances himself, before lifting off with his forehand and planting both hind feet together to push off with them at the moment of take-off. At this point, the head and neck come up and back momentarily as the horse rises to the fence, but then they stretch right out, down and forwards over the fence during the flight, creating a picture of the whole body describing a balanced and beautifully fluid arc called a parabola.

As the horse starts to descend from his maximum height over the fence, the head and neck appear to come back and up again. If he is landing from a big fence, they may well drop right down again quickly as he gets his

As this pony starts his take-off, he begins to stretch out his neck and head

He pushes off with both hind feet level, lifts his forehand, folds his forelegs and arches his head and neck forward

As the pony begins his descent, his head and neck are still stretched out to cope with the change of balance

The hindquarters are now higher than the head as the pony prepares to land with his right fore foot first

balance during the landing. One fore foot will land then the other (depending on which lead you have asked for during the moment of suspension over the fence!) followed by the hind feet, which then push up and off into the getaway.

This description supposes that the rider does not interfere with the horse's jump. Later (in chapter 5 – can you just not wait to get there?!) I deal with the best, most balanced and non-interfering way to sit over a fence in order to allow the horse maximum use of his body so that he can clear the fence for you. Remember, he wants to clear the fence. I am sure that no horse actually enjoys banging his legs on poles or getting them stuck in brushwood although there are some that do appear not to really care.

He leaves the ground with a leap that takes him well over the top. The position of his head and neck show how important it is to give a horse freedom when he is jumping

In full flight, the pony's head and neck are still stretched right out and down

The right fore lands (note the stretch down the back of the leg), followed by the left fore. You can see how important it is to stay off the horse's back during landing

THE HORSE'S BODY WHEN JUMPING

This sequence of photographs shows a little understood point about a jumping horse, emphasizing beyond doubt how crucial it is not to interfere with the head and neck during a jump. Look especially at photos 2 to 6 and compare the position of the pony's head to the fence rail in the background. Note that his head stays in the same plane, more or less level with the rail, throughout all phases of the actual jump, even though he has jumped quite high. As he bascules (arcs) beautifully over the fence, his head acts like a still centre point for balance around which the rest of his body moves. The only way that the rider can permit this is to take the time and trouble to acquire a truly balanced, independent seat with, consequently, no need to prop the hands (which are holding the reins) on the horse's neck or use his mouth as an anchor.

The horse at liberty

Even if they are not perfectly conformed and even if they do not have dead straight action, most horses at liberty are perfectly balanced for what they want to do. How often do you see a horse – with no tack of any kind, and no rider – fall down? Hardly ever unless he slips or trips on rough ground, and even then horses scramble and struggle to their utmost to stay on their feet, as does any sensible prey animal. Sarah, my old Thoroughbred mare, used to perform airborne acrobatics in the field. Sunfishing was one of her favourite moves. She could jump like a stag and used to get amazingly high in the air during these antics. She did sometimes lose her footing when she landed. Then she would get up and look around hurriedly as if to see whether anyone had seen her fall – how embarrassing! – shake herself, snort and carry on grazing as if she felt better for having got it out of her system.

Next time he is in the field, watch your horse with a different eye. Try identifying the footfalls, watching how his head and neck, his back, his hips and his tail all swing easily along when he is free of encumbrances like lungeing gear, a rug or a rider. Look for his back rising and falling in trot and canter. Watch his head and neck in particular and note just how it moves to help balance his body in all gaits.

Try and do some loose jumping with him, either of his own accord, as some horses will, or with some encouragement or training. If you jump him on the lunge, be absolutely certain to give him complete freedom or, better still, get someone else to lunge him this way so you can watch, and see how much he moves, and needs, his head and neck balance naturally and effectively. Get this into your mind's eye so you can visualize the ease and beauty with which your horse can move. Remember these images when you ride and aim to interfere as little as possible but to encourage and allow these movements under saddle.

Most people love watching horses and ponies having fun free in the paddock. This handsome pony is striding out well in a fast canter. Note the voluntary position of his head and neck

'Watching a horse at liberty will emphasize to any perceptive observer how much horses need their heads and necks both to balance themselves and to see where they are going. Horses' heads are very precious to them for these reasons!'

An interesting shot, showing the horse just bringing his head and neck to the left as he starts to turn right. Horses moving at speed do this naturally to balance themselves round turns. The fact that we riders usually try to get them to do the opposite when under saddle is why turns and circles can be difficult for young, green or badly schooled horses because they demand different balance and, therefore, muscle use

There's nothing like a good stretch to limber yourself up

Eyesight

Speaking of watching, I should just like to say a little here on the subject of eyesight. We have known for many years that a horse cannot see straight in front of him when his nose is on or behind the vertical because of how his eyes are made and positioned and how they work. Scientific research has proved this indisputably, and work on the subject continues. The horse needs to raise his head and extend (or poke) his nose somewhat in order to see objects that are approaching him from the front, or which he is approaching – like fences. Even if fences are not involved, it cannot be called logical, fair or even safe riding to prevent him from seeing where he is being asked to go. If his head is held in by the rider, he can only see the ground in front of him for a very few metres, not up ahead. In the field, in play or when cavorting around feeling good, horses will toss their heads and move for a very few strides or seconds with their chins tucked in like this. This is their choice. To force them to go like this during work, whatever their sport or discipline, when they surely need all their faculties, is both inexcusable and unforgivable.

It is not at all necessary to ride or train horses in this bullying way in order to control them, under most normal circumstances, or to get them to 'go correctly' and it was not common practice a generation ago. In fact, in the nose-tucked-in-posture they are not going correctly. All the most respected texts on riding over the ages and right up to the present day (some of these are listed in Further Reading, p.150) state clearly that the horse must work with his poll as the highest point of the neck (a possible exception being stallions with a 'crest' to their necks) and with the front of his face not behind the vertical. Unfortunately, these stipulations are frequently ignored to the detriment of the horse, and this is despite their being set out in the rules of the Fédération Équestre Internationale (FEI), the international governing body for the main equestrian sports.

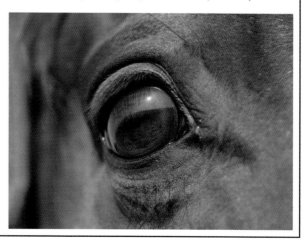

Long and low

During training and physical conditioning of young, inexperienced or spoilt horses, there is a posture called 'long and low', which, again, has become the subject of much misunderstanding and misuse. The object of it is to get the horse to stretch himself along his topline, to work with his back raised, his belly lifted, his hindquarters tilted under and his head and neck stretched out and down. This posture, with the raised back, is a stronger, safer way for the horse to bear weight on his spine than one with a sagging back, head and neck up and out, the pelvis not engaged/flexed under and the hind legs trailing out behind. If this is something you have not considered before, perhaps you would like to try a little experiment, provided that you have no back or other physical problems and entirely at your own risk (see An experiment, p.50).

2. He stretches his neck forward, down and out ...

1. The front of the face comes only just behind the vertical as the horse flexes at the poll

WORKING LONG AND LOW

This lovely horse is being schooled in the famous, or sometimes infamous and often misunderstood, long and low outline with the front of his face only just behind the vertical. This will help him to stretch his topline, without overdoing it and distressing him, and encourage him to raise his back and engage his hindquarters. This gymnastic technique should only be performed for seconds at a time with frequent breaks on a loose rein

3. ... and flexes his hindquarters at the lumbo-sacral joint (at the croup).

4. These actions encourage the belly to lift and the back to rise as the horse learns to round up into the vertebral bow posture (see p.56).

An experiment

Try this experiment to learn a little of how we feel to a horse when we ride and how an incorrect posture – in horse or rider – can affect his reactions and way of going.

· Get down on all fours and give a child a ride on your back.

· To start with arch and hold your back upwards a little and tuck your bottom under slightly, without forcing anything. You will find that this stabilizes your back and the child's weight is fairly easy to tolerate. Ask him or her to sit over your ribcage, not your loins, and to keep still and upright, sitting on the seat bones. Carrying him or her will be easy.

· Now ask the child to flop about and kick you in the ribs as you move around. It is more difficult to balance your load and tolerate the poor riding.

· Next let your back sag down and stick your bottom out instead of under. Your back will feel less stable and will also start to ache pretty soon. Ask your rider to sit correctly and still, and walk around. He or she will feel noticeably heavier.

· Finally, ask him or her to flop about and kick you in the ribs again as you move around. This will be the most difficult of all to tolerate: your back is unstable, your rider feels quite heavy, it was difficult enough to balance your load when it was still but the bad riding makes it really horrible.

This experiment should give you a really good idea of the effects of your own back posture, on how you bear weight and, therefore, why the horse should be encouraged to go with a slightly raised back and tucked-under hindquarters. You'll also get first-hand knowledge of how awful it is for the horse to have to try to balance a bad rider and move, too, particularly when his own back is loose and sagging. If you want to play this horsey game to its ultimate, fit yourself with reins, a bit and a tight noseband plus a tight leather belt around your ribcage, and give the rider *carte blanche* to pull and yank at the reins as well as banging about on your back and kicking you – if he or she dares. Point made, I hope.

TEACHING LONG AND LOW

The 'long and low' exercise helps the horse to develop the right posture and should be used when he is coming on a little and ready for more athletic work to develop his physique. The horse must have learned to go in horizontal balance before you work on long and low, otherwise he will carry too much weight on his forehand, develop 'downhill' balance and stress his forelegs. When doing this exercise the front of the face is brought *only just* behind the vertical (photo on pp.48–49) to bring about a little stretch along the topline, which encourages the horse to adopt the correct posture and develop the right 'riding' muscles in maintaining it. *This only happens if the horse is comfortable and not forced*, otherwise he will resist and use, and therefore develop, the wrong muscles, and will also contort his body to escape the discomfort or pain.

From the ground you can teach your horse to give to gentle but definite, intermittent squeezes from one rein at a time (never sawing at the mouth from side to side), you can then transfer the technique to the saddle. When he can go in self-balance with a nice, forward and swinging action when being ridden, ask him to bring his muzzle *very slightly* behind the vertical with gentle asking squeezes on the inside rein. It is essential that you do not keep up a rigid contact, saw or pull his head in and back. It helps to have a mirror in your school, or a sensible and knowledgeable friend on the ground to tell you when the posture is achieved. As soon as it is, stop asking (applying the squeezes) because he has given you what you want. Sit still and, at first, only expect a very few strides in this posture. If you need to maintain the forward impulsion, ask with your inside leg; again, stop asking when he has responded.

The important points to remember about this technique are that:

1. It must not be forced by any means such as training aids or harsh use of the hands but *requested* by tactful aids, particularly give-and-take on the inside rein once forward energy has been achieved. It must not be requested for more than a few seconds initially as it is hard, muscular work. The horse will gradually develop in strength if it is done correctly but, even then, this is a schooling/strengthening technique only, and, like any gymnastic exercise in human or equine athletic training, is not to be used for more than a very few minutes in any schooling session, with very frequent breaks.

2. The instant the horse gives softly to the bit *the aids must be stopped* so that he comes to understand that complying causes cessation of the request. He will quickly learn to hold the position and go in this way himself *without* being held in it – in other words, going in self-balance – which is just what you want.

3. When he comes out of it, as he will quickly and frequently in the early stages, the aids can be repeated to ask him to resume the posture. It is crucial to be happy with a very little progress over weeks and months, and to err on the side of caution, asking for too little rather than too much. Drilling a horse, overdoing things and forcing him with equipment or harsh riding will distress, sicken and embitter him and can only be described as inhumane.

4. The degree to which the front of the face is brought behind the vertical is very slight, no more than a couple of centimetres depending on the horse's conformation.

5. Done correctly and tactfully with the aim of developing the horse's physique so that he can hold his body in the correct posture, 'long and low' can be beneficial. Otherwise, it causes a lot of harm.

Transitions

Transitions take place between gaits but also within them. They always require a rebalancing from the horse and so are good for getting his weight up and back and the hind legs under. Watch your horse at liberty again – you will notice this if you look for it.

An often overlooked aspect of upward transitions from one gait to another – halt to walk, walk to trot, trot to canter – is that you must 'open the door' in front for the horse to go through, in other words you must give with your fingers to encourage him to go on into the different, faster gait. So many people think that this means that you lose the contact but this is not so. You do not even need to put your hands forward, just to open the fingers of both hands a little to give him a feeling of freedom to move up a gear.

Transitions downwards often result in the rider tipping forward because she is not holding her upper body and lets it continue with the impetus of the previous gait. If you know you have a tendency to tip forwards, consciously hold your upper body very slightly back. Transitions downwards should be relaxed affairs with the body being held upright and controlled but not stiff, and the seat lightened in the saddle. Many people sit more heavily in the saddle for a downward transition, but this can make the horse flatten his back at just the moment when he needs to raise it a little to bring the hind legs forward and the weight back to slow down. Instead, slightly tense your seat muscles, which will raise you a touch in the saddle, and almost lean back. Gently stop moving your hands with the horse's head and neck and he will come down a gait.

Transitions within gaits involve shortening and lengthening strides and moving from, say, collected to medium walk, working to medium trot or medium to collected canter. Any change within a gait is a transition and they are very good for commanding the horse's attention, developing the elasticity of his strides and developing his muscles. The same techniques can be used to ask for them – a slight slowing as described above to shorten the stride, a little encouragement with the inside leg and opening the fingers to lengthen, and so on.

Anne and Lucy demonstrate a poor transition from trot to canter. Lucy lifts her left hind foot at the precise moment of starting canter from trot.

The diagonal pair of legs lifts to come forward for the second beat but Lucy throws up her head and neck and becomes unbalanced

A good walk to halt transition. Anne and Lucy are walking along, with the right lateral pair in support and the left hind just coming forward

Anne asks for halt and instead of striding forward with her left hind, Lucy accepts Anne's aid and puts the foot down next to its opposite pair. Her left fore is lifting to travel forwards but ...

... instead of striding on with it she holds it back ...

... and puts it down just slightly in front of its opposite pair. Although Lucy is balancing her stance by moving her right hind foot, she did not move forward from this halt

Flexion

The horse's spine is nothing like as flexible as we'd like to think, but it can move both laterally and longitudinally (sideways and up and down) a little. The most flexible part of it is the neck (but also the tail). Just because the horse is bending his neck does not mean that he is bending (flexing) his spine at all, which is where a lot of people are mistaken. All healthy, sound horses can turn their heads right round to look directly behind them without moving their backs significantly at all.

LATERAL FLEXION

In equitation, we have decided we want the horse to 'flex' himself around the arc of a bend or circle because we think it looks attractive and is logical. One way we judge this is to see whether or not the hind hooves are landing on the same track as the fore ones. In practice, if we are riding a moderate bend or circle we should just be able to see the corner of the horse's inside eye (mane and forelock permitting) and the edge of the nostril. Putting our outside leg back a little asks the horse not to travel as he is inclined, with his hind feet to the outside of the bend, but to keep them in on the track and following the forefeet. He adjusts his hips and pelvis to do this, which gives the impression that his spine is flexing to the circle. Again, if you watch a horse turning in the field, you will see that he makes little or no effort to flex around a bend other than with his neck. He is more likely to turn like a battleship en bloc and just achieve his direction by placing his feet where he wants to go. This is why circles are difficult for horses, and small ones (10m or less) are quite advanced (note the small 'a') movements in trot and especially canter, particularly if the horse is carrying a poorly balanced or interfering rider.

53

3. The quarters are noticeably flexed under, enabling the hind legs to come forward and both carry weight and thrust the horse forwards with a light forehand.

2. The rider maintains the classic elbow-hand-horse's mouth position with a light, guiding feel on the bit. The horse looks quite comfortable with this.

1. The neck reaches up and forwards. The poll is the highest point and the front of the face is in front of the vertical.

CANTER

A lovely picture of canter. The horse's hindquarters and hind legs are well engaged, his back is up, his neck reaching up and forwards and his nose correctly in front of the vertical. This horse must be giving his rider, who is in a beautifully balanced position, a wonderful feeling. They both look happy

POLL AND JAW FLEXION

The horse's skull is joined to the top of his neck at a vertebra called the atlas. The joint between these, the atlanto-occipital joint, is often called the 'yes' joint because it allows the horse to nod his head. It is what flexes when we ask a horse to flex at the poll. The next joint down the neck is between the atlas and the axis, the atlanto-axial joint. This is often called the 'no' joint because it allows the horse to turn his head from side to side. It is involved in lateral flexions. Another joint involved when the horse is asked to flex or give to the bit is the one just below his ears where the lower jaw joins the skull. This is the 'jaw joint' – the temporomandibular joint – and it needs to flex to open the mouth slightly so that the horse can comfortably accept and gently play with his bit or bits, which is why the current fashion for tightening nosebands as much as possible 'so that the horse cannot evade the bit' creates considerable misery for the horse and has no place in correct, humane, light, harmonious riding.

This is Brodie's first canter in a new place. She is anxious and, although covering the ground, she is not flexing and rounding. Her back is down and her head and neck are up and tense

The traditional and correct standard for poll flexion is that the poll should be the highest point of the horse's neck during work and that the front of the face should be just in front of the vertical when the horse is in collection. Note: in collection. The state of being 'on the bit' is not collection but a stage before it. I prefer to use the older term 'in hand' because it does not imply pressure, which too many riders and trainers are ready to apply to excess. Being 'in hand' calls for the poll flexion to be less than that of collection, which is a more advanced state, so the front of the face should be a little more in front of the vertical. It means that the horse is going 'up to his bridle' and flexing both his poll and his jaw in a comfortably offered, self-maintained posture, gently holding the bit and able to move it in his mouth in a two-way communication with his rider. The head and neck must not be pulled or held in with the neck shortened and the poll over-flexed as this, like a tight noseband, prevents acceptance of the bit. The horse will either resist or tolerate this but will not willingly accept it and cooperate.

Using the reins to communicate

There is no right or wrong way to hold double reins: it depends on your preference. What matters is that you do not confuse the two reins and that you are comfortable.

This shows the most usual way of holding double reins, with the reins crossed so that the bridoon is beneath the ring finger and the curb between the middle and ring fingers. I find this has insufficient finger separation, but that is a personal feeling

My favoured way of holding double reins is with the bridoon between the index and middle fingers and the curb between the ring and little fingers. The upper rein (bridoon) is uppermost in your hand and the lower one (the curb) is lowest

Concentrate on holding your reins, whether single or double, between your index finger and thumb, using your lower fingers to manipulate them. By opening your fingers like this, you can give your horse a significant amount of rein

By closing your fingers you can take or shorten the rein again. This photo shows another way of holding double reins, separated only by the little finger

A classical, inside rein aid to invite the horse to turn. Keeping your elbow at your hip, rotate your wrist out so your fingernails face the sky, and carry your hand inwards a little, as if you were handing someone a plate of soup. This simple technique carries the rein inwards and most horses oblige like magic. If they don't, a little vibration or gentle feel on the rein is enough to confirm what you want

VERTEBRAL BOW AND RING OF MUSCLES

The point of gently teaching and persuading the horse to accept the bit and be 'in hand' is to achieve the effect it has on the rest of his body. His neck will stretch out and forward, his belly and back (spine) will lift in a posture known as the 'vertebral bow' and he will find it easier to engage his hindquarters and hind legs to produce willing and enjoyable, swinging, confident, free, forward movement. He cannot move in this way if he is restricted in the head and neck because the tension, even pain, it creates permeates his entire body. Horses contorted in this way present an artificial, forced and unhappy picture, often producing excessive saliva and froth around their mouths because of their discomfort (excessive salivation being a sign of distress). They may also sweat during work that would barely raise a glow in correctly ridden horses.

To be able to work in the 'vertebral bow' the horse needs to use his 'ring of muscles' which when correctly engaged will produce a strong posture with the spine braced slightly upwards, a little more weight on the hindquarters and hind legs, and a lightening of the forehand. These muscles and their associated structures basically run along and around the horse's top line, pelvis and thighs, along his belly and under his lower neck vertebrae. They enable him to lift and push out his neck, raise his back and belly, and tuck his hindquarters under. (For details on how to achieve this way of going, see pp.74–105.) It is not possible for the horse to activate 'the ring' if his head and neck are pulled or held in.

Lateral work

Lateral work is something at which many owners draw the line. It all sounds too complicated and what is the point of it all? The point of it is to make your horse safer by being more manoeuvrable and to evenly develop his muscles and so his overall strength. Of course, there are many working horses who are never asked to do a side-step under saddle in their lives and they seem fine, but the benefits of judicious lateral work cannot be denied. It improves strength, suppleness, balance and agility so is well worth practising.

Horses do use lateral moves at liberty to position themselves where they want to be, the most obvious movement being a shy away from something that they want to avoid. Clearly, in work, we ask more of them, partly for training and strengthening purposes and partly, in a schooled, made horse, for purposes of display, competition and manoeuvrability.

Turn on (or about) the forehand is usually the first lateral movement to be taught. Basically, the horse lifts his fore feet up and down in a small circle while one hind leg crosses in front of the other to move the hindquarters over. For a turn on the forehand to the right, for instance, the horse is flexed slightly right, looking where he is going and the quarters move to the left, so that he does, in fact, turn to the right.

A turn on the forehand to the right. Lucy's head and neck are flexed slightly right and her right hind is crossing in front of her left. Anne's weight is slightly to the right and her right leg is back a little and around Lucy's side to ask her to move her hindquarters left. Anne often prefers to work without stirrups as do many riders with a deep, established seat

Turn on the haunches

In this attempt at turn on the haunches to the left, Lucy is not engaged and is walking forwards and round instead of keeping her hind feet within a very small circle and bringing her forehand around them

Here, Anne's weight is a little further back and she has a more restraining, but not hard, contact on the bit to remind Lucy not to walk forwards. Lucy, with a good left flexion, picks her hind feet up and down but keeps them within a very small circle while her forelegs move sideways on a circle to bring her forehand round

Shoulder-in is the classic lateral movement and is a good foundation exercise for all others. This can be very slight with the front hooves moving just slightly in off the manège track, or quite pronounced, the horse making four distinct tracks with his hooves. Shoulder-in balances and lightens the horse as he moves his weight back a little on to his hindquarters. It also teaches lateral flexion of the body and supples and strengthens it.

Anne and Lucy in a good shoulder-fore. The position of Lucy's feet coming inwards from the fence is left hind, left fore, right hind and right fore

There is not much difference between shoulder-fore (previous photo) and shoulder-in but it is significant in that it asks for more flexion. Anne and Lucy do a good, three-track shoulder-in here, with the left fore travelling in front of the right hind. Again, Lucy is flexed to the right

Leg yield is another basic lateral movement, which many feel is not so useful as shoulder-in, but which does develop the muscles particularly on the insides and outsides of the limbs from hip and shoulder down. The horse, certainly at first, is flexed slightly away from the direction in which he is being asked to go as this feels easier to him. He crosses both his hind and fore legs in front of their partners to move sideways and diagonally across the ground. Again, this supples and strengthens him and, done properly, is a good gymnastic exercise.

(For information on aids, including those for lateral work, see chapter 8, The aiding system, pp.120–143.)

Shoulder-out is more difficult for the horse as there is not so much psychological support from the fence. This shows a good three-track shoulder-out position, with the horse flexed left and Anne's right rein helping to keep the horse's shoulders out to the left by pressing sideways on the lower part of the neck

Leg yield is a good introduction to lateral movement after turns on the forehand and haunches, to establish the idea of sideways submission to the leg aid. The horse looks away from the direction of movement as this is easier (a flexion towards the direction of movement would be half pass, an advanced movement) and the shoulders should lead slightly, as here

Outside influences

The way a horse moves can be affected by a number of influences, not only a badly balanced rider. It is of little use trying to ride a horse well, kindly and positively if he is in pain. Tack, clothing, teeth, feet, shoes and injuries are all very common causes of horses struggling and resisting, sometimes quite strongly, during work. For your horse to be able to work well, he must be completely comfortable.

Horse and rider equipment

Any item of equipment that makes a horse so uncomfortable he feels the need to avoid its effects will cause him to use the 'wrong' muscles in movement, muscles not meant to be used for that particular movement, unaccustomed and, therefore, weak muscles. This is called 'compensatory movement' because the horse is compensating for being unable to move normally by using other muscles instead. Apart from the physical stress and, quite possibly, injury that this can cause, we must also consider the psychological distress of his having to put up with the sometimes quite severe discomfort. Of course, some horses quite understandably make their discomfort known by playing up, bucking, kicking out, rearing, charging off and various other defensive behaviours. Who can blame them?

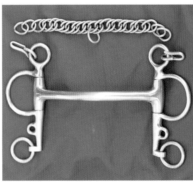

Far left, from top: ported Kimblewick (Kimberwicke) with curb chain; half moon/mullen-mouthed eggbutt snaffle; loose ring French-link snaffle.
Left: half moon/mullen-mouthed, fixed-sided (eggbutt), short-cheeked pelham. The link hanging down from the curb chain is for the lip strap (where used) to pass through
These are good, basic riding bits. Tact and skill are needed most for bits with curb chains. The half-moon snaffle may suit horses that fuss with their mouths and the French-link those that need more mobility

High bits and tight nosebands
The problems with high bits and tight nosebands are:

· the bit is exerting pressure all the time on the corners of the horse's mouth, making it sore and maybe split, but in time calloused and greatly reducing its sensitivity
· the noseband is keeping the mouth tight shut which means that the horse cannot possibly flex his lower jaw (see pp.54–55) to accept the bit but instead is encouraged to resist in a futile effort to get away from this trap

A distressed horse suffering discomfort or pain in his mouth, shown by his unhappy expression and the attitude of his muzzle. This could be caused by his bit and/or the way it is used, or he could have dental or other mouth problems. His throatlatch is too tight and the bit appears to be rather high in the mouth. The flash strap on his noseband could also be too tight for comfort

Check the bridle fits

- Can you slide a finger *easily* all round under all the straps of your horse's bridle, including under every part of the noseband, if used?

- The headpiece must not cut into the back of the ears. For horses where the headpiece tends to slip up to the back of the ears, it is worth trying a 'cut-away' headpiece, available from some saddlers.

- The cheekpieces must not rub the area around the eyes or come anywhere near the eyes.

- The noseband must not rub the facial bones.

- The throatlatch should be loose enough to allow you to fit the width of your hand between it and the round jawbone, and should lie halfway down the latter. If the throatlatch is tighter than this, the horse will sense it, even if he cannot feel it, and this is enough to prevent him wanting to flex to the bit.

Lucy wearing her very well-fitted pelham bridle. There is plenty of room around her ears with the browband long enough to allow the headpiece to sit back but not so long that it flops about. The throatlatch and noseband are comfortably loose and the noseband is below the facial bones so as not to rub them. The bit fits snugly into the corners of her mouth, just creating a slight wrinkle. The curb chain is lying well down in her chin/curb groove. Lucy is a chunkily built horse and, you will have noticed, finds it difficult to flex much at the poll, so is not asked for more than a slight flexion. Because of her excellent schooling, she is nevertheless well-balanced and light to ride

'The basic guideline for well-fitting tack is that, above all, it must be comfortable.'

This throatlatch should be a little looser to allow the horse more room to flex at the poll, and the bit appears to be a little too high

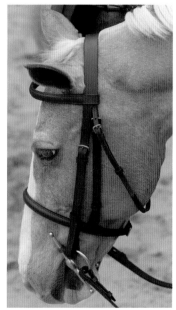

This browband is too big but, despite that, the headpiece is cutting into the backs of the ears. The throatlash is comfortably loose and the bit the correct height. The loops on the bit's upper cheeks are fitted to the bridle cheekpieces to keep them still, which will steady the bit in the mouth

Check bit and curb chain

Although the horse's teeth may decide how a bit should be adjusted, in normal mouths the following applies:

- A jointed snaffle bit should create one wrinkle only at the corners of the lips.

- A half-moon/mullen mouthpiece – whether snaffle, pelham or curb – should comfortably touch the corners of the lips but create no wrinkles, or a small one at most.

- With a double bridle, the bridoon should fit as described for a snaffle (above) and lie over the top of the curb bit in the mouth. The curb or Weymouth should lie about 1cm (½in) below the bridoon, so it must not touch the corners of the lips at all.

- You should be able to fit the width of one finger between the horse's face and the bit's cheek or ring; if not, the bit is too narrow, if more, the bit is too wide.

- A curb chain must lie flat and smooth down in the curb or chin groove. It must not lie or ride up on the jawbones where it can rub and will not have the correct effect. You should be able to slide one finger under it all the way around: it should be just so tight that it allows the cheeks of the bit to be brought back to 45 degrees with the line of the lips.

Sky's curb chain lies correctly, well down in his chin/curb groove. He does not wear a cover or lip strap. Many people find that a lip strap can adversely affect the position and movement of the chain

This curb chain is lying too high up. It could rub the thin skin of the jawbones and is also twisted so will be causing the horse discomfort or even pain

This Western curb chain is fitted rather loose. This will result in the bit shanks having to be pulled back quite a way before the chain acts, which will alter the lie of the bit in the mouth. If it is a ported bit, the port may press painfully into the roof of the horse's mouth as a result

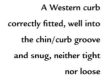

A Western curb correctly fitted, well into the chin/curb groove and snug, neither tight nor loose

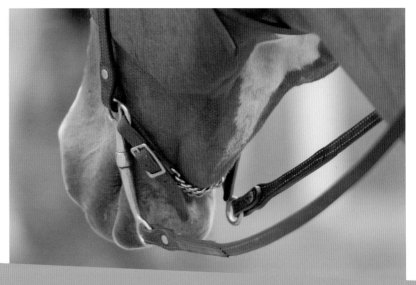

Check the saddle fits

• Can you quite easily slide the flat of your fingers all round under the edges of your saddle? Ensure that it is neither too tight in front so that it pinches and bruises your horse, nor too wide so that it rocks from side to side, which also causes bruising. Remember that a numnah may temporarily help the fit of a too-wide saddle but will make a tight one feel even tighter.

• Can you see a clear tunnel of daylight all down the spine when the horse's heaviest rider is mounted?

• Does the saddle create an even bearing surface on the horse's back, spreading pressure as much as possible? At the back, ensure that the saddle does not press into the back muscles. In the middle, you must not be able to notice an easing of the pressure. This indicates that the saddle is 'bridging' on the horse's back, creating too much pressure in front and at the back but not enough in the middle. Some deeply gusseted saddles can cause problems at the back by presenting too flat a panel under the seat (with the idea of creating stability on the back) and pressing into the muscles under the cantle.

• The saddle should be positioned so that you can fit the edge of your hand between the back of the shoulder blades at the top (just behind the withers) and the front edge of the saddle. If it is further forward than this it can interfere with the action of the shoulders, tilt the saddle out of balance and cause the rider to sit too near the cantle

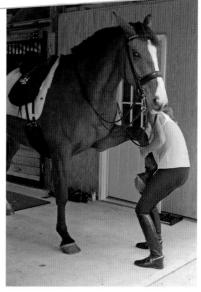

Although it is good to smooth out the skin beneath the girth by pulling the forelegs forward, this should be done moderately as the object is only to smooth out any wrinkles and prevent a pull on the skin when the legs come forward in movement, which can discourage horses from moving freely

and pull the girth into the backs of the elbows, all of which prevent comfortable, good riding.

• The loins (and, of course, the spine all the way from pommel to cantle) must be free from contact, never mind actual pressure.

• Girths should lie ideally at least a hand's width behind the point of the elbow so as not to dig in here, and should be evenly elasticated, at both ends or in the middle, to allow the horse some room to expand his ribcage and to breathe comfortably. Elastic at one end only causes the saddle to be pulled to the opposite side when the horse breathes in, and back again when he breathes out.

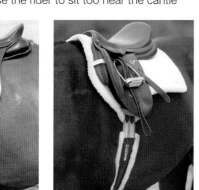

A dressage saddle of good width and length for the horse, placed far enough back to clear the tops of the shoulder blades at the withers but to avoid the loins. It has a correctly adjusted numnah, pulled well up into the gullet. This horse does not have a natural girth groove to help hold the girth in place, but it lies just far enough back to avoid interfering with the action of the elbows

Close contact jumping saddles need skilled fitting, otherwise they can cause wither pressure when the rider's weight is forward over a fence. Thick padding only lessens pressure, it does not remove it and makes a tight saddle tighter as it takes up room beneath the panel. This girth seems to be lying too close to the elbow

This saddle is rather too low over the withers although it is well placed and the girth is far enough back from the elbow

Going to the other extreme is this dressage saddle which seems unnecessarily high in the pommel. It is well placed and the girth lies well back from the elbow. (In some saddles, a high pommel is an indication that the saddle is too narrow and perching on the back: in such cases, thick padding makes the saddle feel even tighter by taking up space under the panel.)

Training aids and devices of all kinds must not be used to in any way force a horse into what the trainer feels is the correct posture. If used at all, they must be adjusted to encourage the horse to maintain a natural posture and only come into effect when, for instance, his head rises above the point of control or a beneficial posture (see below).

On close inspection this lungeing scene reveals several faults. The most obvious is the side reins, which are too short, forcing the horse into an overbent posture. The roller is too far forward, hampering the action of the shoulders and forelegs, and the trainer is restricting the size of the circle yet sending the horse on too fast. The horse makes his feelings plain with his facial expression

Correctly fitted side reins can be useful to 'advise' a horse of a comfortable and beneficial position for his head and to increase control with difficult horses. When used during lungeing before riding, the horse should first be worked for several minutes with a free head and neck, the side reins only being applied (no shorter than this) when the horse has warmed up enough to start being asked to come into hand or outline

These running reins are in their potentially most severe setting, passing from the rider's hand, through the bit rings, down between the horse's forelegs and fastening to the girth. Running reins, often called draw reins, have a powerful head-lowering effect but also often bring the muzzle behind the vertical depending on how strongly they are used and can easily put the horse's weight too much on to his forehand. However, here they are very loose and are clearly not in use all the time. If used with great tact, and only when needed, they can serve a temporary purpose in schooling horses who habitually go with their heads up and their noses out. Such horses should be checked for discomfort in the back and mouth particularly, which often causes that way of going

CLOTHING

You may ask: how can clothing possibly affect a horse's action? After all, he does not wear it when being ridden (apart from maybe an exercise sheet). The point is that horses often wear clothing for many hours at a time. Any constriction it causes can make restricted movement a habit and actually hamper natural muscle development, so badly fitting rugs can hinder action in quite a significant way. They are also very uncomfortable for horses, and cause psychological stress for this reason.

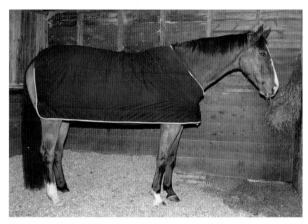

This rug is a little too small for this horse and is not leaving enough room for his shoulders

In my experience and from my observations, there is no doubt that horses are far happier and more comfortable without any rugs at all, under normal circumstances, other than when out in very wet, windy or cold weather, or as protection from insects in warm weather. Nowadays, most horses are forced to wear far too many rugs; and some people persist with the tradition of piling on rugs in the mistaken belief that it will hasten casting of the winter coat. In fact, this is brought about mainly by increasing day length, so better results would be achieved by leaving on the lights (see Further Reading, p.150).

Check the rug fits

• Does it come well forward of the withers, without creating any pull around the neckline or on the points of the shoulders? The points of the hips and the croup are other areas where lack of space in the design creates pulling and pressure.

• Do the design devices, such as pleating and darts, to shape the rug to the horse allow for very free movement of the legs, bearing in mind that horses move naturally from shoulder and hip, not merely elbow and stifle. So many rugs have pleats that stop at the tops of the forelegs. This is better than none at all but does nothing to permit freedom of the shoulder.

This purple outdoor rug looks well used, roomy and comfortable. The horse's Shetland pony friends don't need rugs

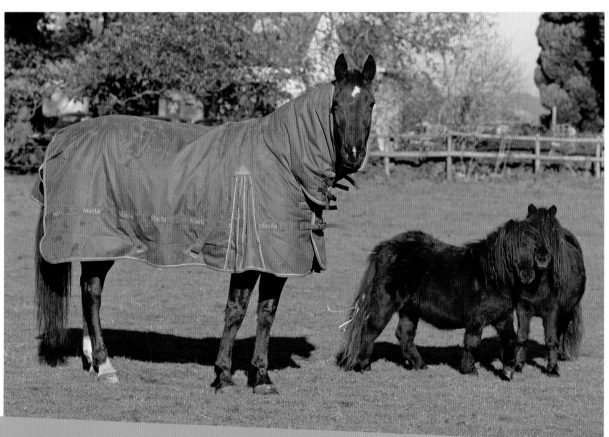

Farriery

Although a horse's sensitive feet are encased in insensitive horn, they are still very susceptible to discomfort and pain. It is very important for everyone concerned with looking after or working horses to cultivate a sixth sense when it comes to a horse's freedom of movement and his apparent comfort or discomfort. It is not simply a case of being able to recognize when a horse is actually lame. Although horses and ponies come in all sorts of shapes and sizes, there is, among them all, a certain freedom and ease of movement that disappears quickly when an animal is even slightly uncomfortable in its feet.

Most horses can be shod to good effect by a skilled and conscientious farrier. Some horses are also genuinely comfortable and able to work well without shoes when their feet are skilfully trimmed and of sound constitution. Many others, though, are not, even though their owners would like them to be, or may even tell themselves that they are. The most important aspects of foot care are:

• To be absolutely honest with yourself about what your horse needs

• To pull out all the stops to fulfil those needs, whether or not they fit in with your ideas of farriery, foot care and management. Different types of shoes and shoeing systems, and trimming and trimming systems, come and

A well-shod foot, equally balanced from side to side, with the two visible ends of the coronet at equal heights to the ground

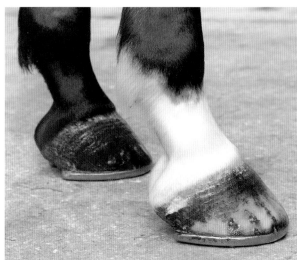

Well-balanced and shod feet, with the foot/pastern axis (the toe and front of the pastern) on the same angle or line, and well supported at the heels. The heels are sloped at the same angle as the toe

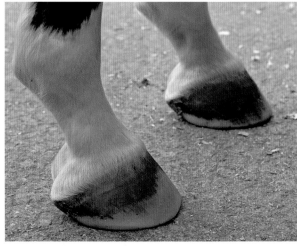

Strong-looking, well-balanced and neatly trimmed unshod feet

go and – is this just a peculiarity of the horse world, I wonder? – some people seem to jump on anything new (not just in farriery) as though it were the Holy Grail, and put it into effect, whether or not it suits their horses.

Study equine action and, most importantly, body language, minutely and try to get a real feel for whether or not a horse is uncomfortable or, conversely, is moving completely comfortably, freely and happily. Stand back and look at his demeanour, action and, particularly, his face and ears: horses' faces are very expressive and the way they hold their bodies also tells us whether they are protecting themselves from discomfort or pain or moving naturally and comfortably. (Learn from watching your horse at liberty, too, see p.46.)

Legs which swing outwards, like this, are less serious a fault than those which swing inwards towards the opposing leg

Horses that carry their feet inwards like this are at risk of tripping and of injuring the opposing leg of the pair

Injuries – old and new

Any athletic horse or human will, sooner or later, sustain an injury. In fact, the less fit you are the more likely it is that you will become injured because you are out of condition. Any sudden movement or unaccustomed activity or work, such as a longer-than-usual hack for your horse or digging the garden for you, can cause muscle and other soft tissue (non-bone) stress and perhaps strain. Horses are mammals just like us and, again like us, feel pain in exactly the same way but they cannot ask you for a couple of painkilling tablets or tell you that they aren't able to work today because they are in pain somewhere. Again, studying body language can help you here.

Just because an old injury has healed it does not mean that the horse no longer feels its effects. A poorly treated muscle injury or tendon sprain, for instance, can cause long-term changes in action, shortened stride, altered gait and reluctance on the part of the horse to use that part. Soft tissue, when healing, forms fibrous scar tissue ('replacement' tissue), which is not so elastic or strong as the original tissue. This can cause lack of suppleness (looseness) and, therefore, flexibility in action. Also, a problem with incorrectly managed injuries is that adhesions can form; these cause previously separate tissues to 'stick' (adhere) to each other. When work is resumed, adhesions can tear apart, re-injuring the area. Such problems can be avoided or greatly lessened with good physical therapy from your vet or a physiotherapist or other equine bodyworker, as appropriate.

Chronic (long-lasting) pain or discomfort from old injuries will affect the way a horse moves, as he will try to do so without feeling the pain. Lameness is an obvious symptom when the horse tries to take the weight off the painful limb and bear more of it on the sound, non-painful one. Back injuries are often more complex: actual lameness may not be present but the horse is clearly very uncomfortable. Then there are diseases, such as osteoarthritis, which can spell the end of a horse's career.

New injuries can cause acute pain (pain of recent origin) and must be correctly treated and given time to heal if the horse's physical abilities are to be regained. The horse may then need careful work to rebuild his fitness.

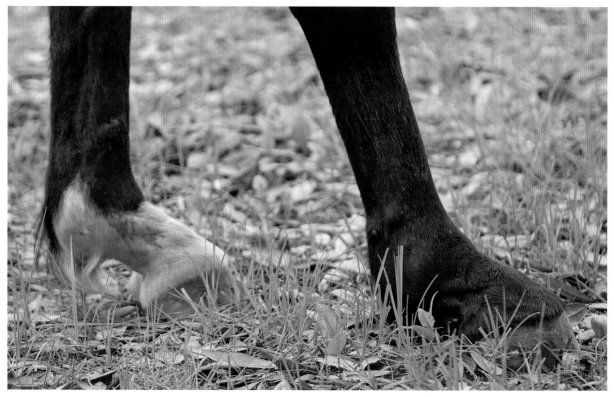

This horse has had an injury that has weakened the tendons and ligaments, allowing the fetlock to drop. Such injuries can significantly affect a horse's ability to work. The fetlock in this horse is also permanently enlarged due to tissue damage: such horses find work on soft surfaces very difficult. However, if, due to wear and tear, the joints are also damaged and arthritic, work on hard surfaces is also out of the question

Poor riding

I have already said a lot on the effects that poor riding can have on a horse's way of going. It can also change a horse's gaits long-term. As a shiatsu therapist, I have found that the main problems are from riders pulling their horses' heads in, either with the reins or some gadget, and causing them to be overbent, which almost always has the effect of 'squashing' in the neck – shortening it and causing compression in the throat area, which affects the breathing, and creates soft tissue tension and pain in the head, poll, neck, shoulders and back. The fact that the horse is made to move, often in a very exaggerated way, without the use of his head and neck to help his movement and to balance his body and his rider causes even more discomfort and pain.

Horses that are treated like this often develop the habit of moving with a very stiff head, neck and back, with no swing to the body, no freedom and elasticity of movement, but with unnaturally exaggerated extensions and 'lift' to the action which, to someone who understands and is familiar with the beauty of natural action and has a love of the horse, is not only ridiculous but also distressing to watch. This is how gaits begin to be destroyed. Earlier in this chapter I talked about compensatory movement in relation to tack and clothing. Horses also use it when restricted by their riders. The muscles a horse learns to use to compensate for this restriction develop over time and so the horse builds up the sort of physique that enables him to cope with this appalling treatment.

'Remember, a horse cannot move well and without discomfort and stiffness, and even pain, somewhere in his body without the free use of his head and neck.'

Rehabilitation is perfectly possible if such a horse is managed and ridden by a balanced rider who can adapt her movements to those of the horse (see chapter 5, again, pp.74–105) and go with him. The horse can then move naturally and, in less time than you imagine, the right muscles will develop at the expense of the others.

I have ridden many such horses – including horses that have worked at the highest levels of competition. Initially, when allowed a freer head and neck and gentler (but not sloppy) seat, they are quite confused because they have nothing to brace against and even have problems balancing. Even if the owner is reluctant to allow me to adjust the tack so it fits more comfortably, it only takes about 20 minutes for most horses to get the hang of a better way of going and start moving more freely, naturally and correctly. Crucially for lightness, the horse will acquire the abilities to move with less stress and more ease and to balance himself under saddle. This means that the rider can concentrate on adapting her movements to those of the horse and to using her body only to give aids. To the horse, this new, much-improved way of being ridden must be like sprouting wings.

'The method of riding I use and teach relies largely on the natural aids of seat, legs and weight rather than on holding the head in a vice-like grip and steering the horse with the reins. Horses understand it naturally and are comfortable with it, so are able to concentrate on what I am asking rather than on resisting me or tolerating the discomfort.'

ARE YOU COMFORTABLE?

Finally, check your own comfort. If you are in pain, experiencing stiffness or weakness or any other physical obstacle to moving well, your riding will never be as good as it could be. Your muscles work just like those of your horse. If you are uncomfortable due to badly fitting clothing or a pinching saddle, you will, consciously or otherwise, try to avoid the discomfort with resulting compensatory movement and lack of concentration on your riding. Make sure that you and your horse are very comfortable in every way – then you really will start to make real progress.

4

How you move

As fellow mammals, the horse's and the human's bodies are both designed around the same basic biological pattern. Clearly there are differences, the most obvious being that the horse is a quadruped, moving on four feet, and with a horizontal format to his body like most mammals. Humans are vertical bipeds, meaning we move on two feet, our other two having evolved to become hands. We have a collarbone, which the horse does not; we also have five digits on each hand and each foot and the horse has only one for practical purposes of locomotion. Over millions of years, our various bones have, in some cases, acquired somewhat different shapes, but we still have a lot in common.

The spine

As an upright animal, our backs experience different stresses from those of horizontal animals but the basic structure and function is the same. Our spine has 24 vertebrae and is the foundation of our bodies. Together the vertebrae form a channel or conduit that houses the spinal cord, from which run the main branches of our nervous system, spreading out all over the body. Nerve impulses, which allow us to sense our environment and know what is happening to us and enable us to move our bodies, travel to and from our brains along the spinal cord.

The vertebrae have pads of protective gristle (cartilage) between them, which absorb jarring and pressure from movement such as locomotion and bending. Most of the muscles of our chest and tummy are at some point connected to the spine. Known as our 'core' muscles, these are especially important for riders; strong core muscles, capable of being held in a state of slight contraction (tone, see also p.15), are needed for good posture of the whole body and for stability of the upper body when riding. Poor, slouched posture means that the core muscles are slack and cannot do their job.

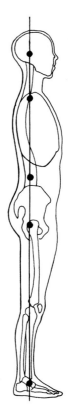

A diagram showing good human posture on the ground. The vertical line drops straight down through the body, passing through the ear, shoulder, small of the back, hip joint and ankle. The small of the back is in its natural slight curve, neither hollowed nor flattened. The pelvis is in a neutral position, not tilting either way. What we call the seat bones are the very bottom of the pelvis

POSTURE

The spine is not straight but gently undulates (see diagram above). This shape is quite adaptable but even though you may be told to 'sit up straight' or to 'flatten your back', if you have a normal spine it will never be either straight or flat. Back pain is rampant in the modern human body which, in many cases, spends most of its time sitting down – a position that places a great deal of stress on the lower back. This is unfortunate because correct functioning of the lower back is absolutely crucial to good riding. Apart from causing weak muscles that are more prone to stress and injury, poor posture – a slumped attitude, hunched shoulders and a generally floppy, downward, compressed inclination to the spine – can cause digestive problems, poor liver function, allergies, emotional problems (many believe), headaches, general weakness, respiratory problems, painful and debilitating nervous problems, poor movement and other disorders. All these are connected to the fact that the spinal cord and the branching nerves are affected by the compression and distortion brought about by bad posture. Poor posture, whether we are sitting, standing or moving, also necessitates unconscious compensatory movement as other muscles try to keep the body upright and in balance.

'If you spend a lot of time slumped over a desk ... your breathing, so essential to life and health, becomes shallow, your energy saps due to lack of oxygen and removal of carbon dioxide and your health will eventually suffer.'

• **Sitting** If you spend a lot of time sitting down slumped or hunched over a desk or computer, your spine experiences compression even if you don't feel pain, and this can weaken your core muscles. Your breathing, so essential to life and health, becomes shallow, your energy therefore saps due to lack of oxygen and inefficient removal of carbon dioxide and your health will eventually suffer. At least try to use an ergonomically designed chair for the sake of your back and, therefore, your health. In general, sit up and well back into your chair, with your shoulders back and down, your head upright, your neck pressed gently back a little and your spine held naturally, or if you are slightly 'hollow backed', with your spine at the waist slightly pressed back against the back of your chair, which should be designed and adjusted to support it.

• **Standing** When standing, do not habitually rest one leg or lean on something. Avoid standing with your hips forward of your ankles so that when viewed from the side, your legs slope – a very common stance. Standing with your feet slightly apart and your weight spread evenly on them enables you to stand comfortably for much longer than you would otherwise. Gently stretch your spine upwards to your head, which should be directly on top of it, not tilting forward or sideways. Your shoulders should be slightly held back and down and your breastbone slightly lifted. Another refinement, which adds strength to your spine and reduces pressure in the lumbar region (the loins or the small of the back), is to slightly tuck your bottom under – note: just slightly. This whole posture is what is called good bearing.

This very poor posture in the saddle is extremely common, and not particularly exaggerated here! The rider is sitting back on her buttocks, looking down at the horse (who does not look very happy about it) with her head jutting forward. Her arms are straight which is pulling her shoulders down and forwards and hollowing her chest. Her legs are too far forward and altogether this presents a very unbalanced, insecure and ineffective position

This is only slightly less common. The rider is perched on her 'fork', tipping forwards, arms again straight and her legs too far back. She is quite out of balance

Practise standing like this until it becomes second nature to you. It should not be forced, but you do have to push yourself a little and keep trying, otherwise nothing will change. Body and muscle strength are all about good, controlled posture and movement. It is quite possible to hold yourself in good bearing and to relax at the same time. Stiffness, force, rigidity and undue tension are bad for your spine and for your whole body and general health. Chapter 7, Mind power, pp.112–119, gives some simple ideas and exercises to assist you in the development and maintainenance of good posture and movement, and some techniques or modalities, which will help you more than you could ever imagine. They will enable you to become stronger, more controlled and deliberate in your movements and posture, and more energetic and more upbeat in your attitudes and emotions. All this will help you both on the ground in your everyday life and, most certainly, on your horse.

Movement

In chapter 2, I described how a horse moves and how his back dipped as each hind leg lifted and rose again as it landed (p.36). A very similar thing happens to your body when you move. As you walk, when your left leg leaves the ground your left hip dips, rising again as your leg lands, while your right leg pushes off and your right hip dips. From the back, this can create, in some people, a noticeable 'wiggle' when they walk – in both sexes. Practise the following way of walking until you do it out of preference. You will feel stronger, more impressive and attractive. Once you get used to it, you will also feel that you can walk much further, are better balanced and both stronger and steadier on your feet.

• **Walk tall** Stand with your spine and head stretched up and your shoulders back and down as described on p.71, the bottom of your pelvis (your pubic bone) tilted a forward a little and your ankles and hips on a vertical line with each other. Relax into your posture and hold it, then simply take one step forward, but do not land your foot in front of the other one like a catwalk model. Walk so that your feet make two tracks close together. Most people turn their toes out a little, some a lot, but ideally try to have your toes pointing straight forward. Hold yourself up with a proud, confident attitude and walk straight forward. As you get used to good posture and straight walking (if you have not been doing it before), walk a little faster and let your arms swing naturally.

• **Bend from the hips** Another common habit, one that is definitely not good for you, is to bend down from the waist to pick things up, whether it is your horse's feet or something you have dropped. This puts a good deal of stress on the spine. If you have ever had a soft-tissue back injury you will have found that bending down like this is so painful that you cannot do it.

Put a book on your head

An old-fashioned trick – that really works to help you develop good posture – is to walk with a book on your head. In countries where women transport huge containers of liquids and baskets of various foods on their heads, can you imagine what would happen if they did not carry themselves straight and controlled? And have you ever noticed what superb, impressive posture these women have, even when they are not carrying anything on their heads? Picture that in your mind's eye, put a book on your head and walk. Make it a good habit.

The best way to bend down is to bend from the hips, not the waist. Flatten your back rather than rounding it, and stick your bottom out a little and you will take the stretch and stress off your back. If you want to reach something on the floor, ideally bend your knees and squat with your back straight, to the side of whatever you want to pick up, then push up with your knees to stand up again. Even if you have a back injury, it is often possible to do this without pain, and it will certainly help to ensure that you don't get one.

What's this got to do with riding? You will find that these ways of standing and moving are important when you learn how to move with your horse when riding at all gaits (see pp.74–105).

It is better for your back if you use your knees to bend down and pick up things from the ground

Standing and riding

It is often said that a good, classical seat in the saddle is more like standing up over your horse than sitting down, and this is true. The good, standing posture described on p.71 is just like that you should adopt when sitting in the saddle with only three changes.

When you get on your horse (from a mounting block or similar, please, for the sake of his back, your back, his mind and your saddle), the only differences in your posture should be that:
  your elbows bend,
  your hips and knees bend,
  your ankles become more flexed as your weight drops down through your heels.

• Do not force your heels down or your toes up as this causes stiff legs due to muscle contraction. In this kind of riding we want tone, not stiffness.

• Just allow the weight of your legs (each leg is 25 per cent of your total body weight) to drop down into your heels, the weight being taken partly down the inside of your thighs and partly on the balls of your feet in the stirrups. Dropped legs draw your seat down into the saddle so that you can drape your seat and legs down around your horse rather than perching on him.

• Do not sit heavily as this can make a horse dip his back down, which you certainly do not want.

• Do use stirrups that feel comfortable: there are several designs that move with and support your feet so try a few.

• **Elbows** – another point to think about. When you are standing up, you do not have your elbows and arms angled out in front of your body unless you are pushing a supermarket trolley or a pram or something. Yet so very many people ride like this, with slouched shoulders, hollowed chest and also bobbing backwards and forwards with the horse's movement. Ride with your elbows by your hips, where they are when you stand – at least most of the time. Bend your elbows to bring your forearms up and hold the reins with your arms in that position and your thumbs on top.

You'll find that good posture, whether you are standing on the ground, sitting on your horse or using a half-seat or forward seat (light seat and slightly forward position of the upper body) for fast work and jumping, becomes effortless as your muscles, particularly your core muscles, become stronger and your balance better.

Read on, the next chapter – yes, chapter 5, you're nearly there – explains how to sit in the saddle and adapt your movements to go with those of your horse while retaining your own correct posture. Like any activity, the more you do it the easier it becomes and eventually it becomes second nature.

How to move together

5

Most people who care about horses and are deeply involved with them have at one time or another marvelled at the sight of a sound, healthy and happy horse moving at will in a field. It is wonderful to watch horses playing, cavorting and performing all sorts of gymnastic feats, all of which make it perfectly obvious that they do not need us to show them how to move. Rather, we need them to show us how to stay with them. To this sort of person, it is also obvious that when a human sits on a horse and tries to influence his movements, all too often the magic is lost.

Why is this? It is because the rider is an interfering burden on the horse's natural balance and action. As well as the physical handicaps of the rider's weight on his back and influencing his actions, the horse has the psychological problem of coping with the loss of freedom of movement.

The only ways humans can get around these major blockages are:
• To learn to ride in such a way that we do not interfere with the horse's natural movement
• To make the process of being ridden comfortable and enjoyable for the horse.

This means that we must:
• Adapt the movements of our seat (buttocks and legs) so that we move with the horse's back
• Teach the horse to use his spine in the 'vertebral bow' posture with his 'ring of muscles' (p.56) fully functioning
• Do absolutely nothing that causes the horse any discomfort, pain or distress either through poor use of our body and aids or by encumbering him with equipment which causes that state.

> ### 'A rider should not be allowed to do anything on a horse until he is capable of doing nothing.'

This well-worn saying is sadly currently having a bit of a rest. It means do nothing to hamper the movement and balance of the horse. To do this, the rider has to be able to control her body, to move it to 'mirror', adapt to or absorb the body movements of the horse – whichever term you prefer. If the horse's back dips on one side, such as when the hind leg lifts, that side of the rider's seat must dip with it. If the horse's back rises, such as in the suspension phase of trot, the rider's seat must rise with it. If the horse

A beautifully balanced seat, appropriate for halt, walk, sitting trot and canter. The traditional sign of a good position is when you are able to draw a straight, vertical line from the rider's ear, through her shoulder and elbow/hip through her ankle or down the back of her heel

is rocking along in a natural, bounding canter stride, the rider must keep her weight, via her seat, still and stable by keeping her upper body upright, absorbing the horse's movement by means of the flexibility of her lower back and hips. If the horse is jumping, the rider must stay in balance with him (being neither too far forward nor too far back) and must allow him to take her hands down with his mouth as he makes his arc or parabola over the fence (pp.44–45).

Not everyone has naturally good coordination, but most people can learn to adapt to the horse's movements if they relax their minds and bodies and do not try so hard that they become anxious and remain tense (see chapters 6 and 7 for information on overcoming these problems). Anxiety and tension can be caused by a rider trying too hard and by nervousness. This second reason is why it is really important, when learning anything new, to have a horse you trust. Lunge lessons with an open-minded teacher can be helpful or, perhaps better, a session with a knowledgeable, interested friend who is happy to just lunge the horse quietly and let you practise to your heart's content. Lungeing, though, is not essential. It is quite possible, when you have a cooperative, well-behaved horse, to teach yourself to move with his movements. Take your time, relax mentally and physically and practise the following techniques.

The ideal way to acquire an independent seat is on the lunge without stirrups or reins. Most of the best riding academies in the world have traditionally lunged their students in this way for months, or as long as it takes, to establish the correct seat and balance before allowing them to ride independently

How to sit on your horse

Bearing in mind what has already been said about the correct fit and positioning of your saddle, and about how the equine and human bodies move, the following description is how to sit on a horse to best effect. The correct seat provides the following benefits to you and your horse:

• You will have a strong, balanced posture and a 'moulding', adapting seat and legs
• You will be secure and confident because you are less likely to fall off
• You will be able to give quiet, effective aids which your horse will understand
• You will make few or no other movements – 'white noise' – which the horse has to sort out from real aids. When you give an aid your horse will know you mean something

YOUR LOWER BODY AND LEGS

Lower yourself gently into the saddle (never land with a flop or a bang) and, with both feet out of the stirrups and legs hanging down, *completely relax the muscles of your buttocks and legs* so that if someone lifts a leg away from your horse's side it flops lifelessly back. It may help you to acquire this level of relaxation if you imagine that you are unable to use your body from the hips downwards. This is a temporary technique to help you realize just how loose

> ### Saddle
>
> For flatwork, you need a saddle that allows you to sit in and maintain the seat described without throwing you out of balance. Many dressage saddles and some others fit the bill, although not specialized jumping saddles. The stirrup bars must be far enough back to allow you to sit in the central dip of the saddle on your seat bones with your legs hanging comfortably down, not pulled forward. This would incline your seat towards the back of the saddle and put you out of balance. A well-designed saddle for flatwork and maybe small obstacles will have the lowest part of the seat in the centre of the saddle, midway between the pommel and the cantle.

you need to be able to make your seat and legs when required. The ability to completely loosen your seat and legs is what enables you to let them move with your horse and adapt to his movements so that it appears to an onlooker, and feels to your horse, as though you are doing nothing. This apparently magical ability, which is a feature of the best classical riders and which causes so much wonderment in the uninitiated, is all down to posture, balance and relaxation – and you can learn it if you are willing to try, and put your mind to it. It is not that difficult.

Normally, your leg muscles will be held slightly toned and the hip, knee and ankle joints relaxed and controlled, so that you can keep your legs easily in position and give aids as needed. Toned does not mean stiff and gripping. Those states will make you insecure and easily dislodged as the horse's body will have something to push against – it is much easier to throw a stone than a jelly.

> ## 'It is much easier to throw a stone than a jelly.'

When you are quite relaxed, feel with your seat for your seat bones, the lowest part of your pelvis (see diagram, p.70), and sit on them rather than more on your buttocks. Just allow your legs to drape down and around your horse's sides, not pressing on. This relaxed position on the seat bones, with your buttocks and legs moulded across your saddle and down your horse's sides is the key to

security and effective aids. Don't take up your stirrups yet; let your toes hang naturally downwards.

YOUR UPPER BODY

Now imagine *stretching* up gently but definitely from your waist and *dropping* down from your waist. Think of your torso as two halves – the top half belongs to you and the bottom half to your horse. As you stretch up, all the way to the top of your head, do not hollow your back as this will make you stiff and give you backache. Instead, very slightly flatten your back in the loin area and gently hold this posture. Hold your shoulders back and down, raise your breastbone a little and push the top of your head up gently. Don't jut out your chin. The back of your neck should be pressed lightly backwards. Now you've got the posture, let your body get the feel of it and store it in its natural memory bank. (This should all be familiar from what you read earlier about good human posture, pp.70–73.)

The test of whether or not a rider can completely relax her leg is to have someone lift it sideways away from the saddle and then let it go, when it should flop lifelessly back again

Keep your upper body in place by holding its muscles in slight tone so that the horse's movements cannot swing it out of place. Get a friend to push you forward between the shoulders and backward on the breastbone. She

'Think of your torso as two halves – the top half belongs to you and the bottom half to your horse.'

should not be able to move you from your upright position, not because you are as rigid as a ramrod but because you are holding your upper body independently, firmly but easily, with little effort, in this elegant, secure posture. Tone takes little energy to maintain whereas stiffness, rigidity and undue tension take a lot. This is why, when you ride using the method described in this book, you do not become anything like so tired as you do when you try other methods.

YOUR ARMS AND HANDS

While your body is committing to memory that posture and 'hold', think about your arms and hands. Let your upper arms just fall straight down to your hips so that your elbows rest, and normally stay, lightly there. Of course, they may need to move from there sometimes but, generally, this is their 'headquarters' or 'default' position. Hold your hands with the little finger at the bottom and your thumb on top (no pushing prams or typing) and hold the reins, which are passing up through your hands, between your thumb and index finger with a light pressure. There is absolutely no need to grip.

With this holding position and technique, you can open your other fingers and give the horse a good few centimetres (up to two or three inches) of rein, or close them and take that much, *without moving your hands or arms, including your elbows*, at all. The knack to good riding is to be as still as possible and to do as little as possible. Think minimalist.

• Carrying your hands flat (pram-pushing/typing) reduces your feel and sensitivity

A good hand position, in which there is a straight line from the elbow, through the hand to the horse's mouth. It is easier to maintain a balanced seat if your elbow is habitually held at the hip with your upper arm dropping down naturally

• Carrying your elbows in front of your hips (and some people really exaggerate this) brings the shoulders forward with them, drops or hollows the chest and causes backwards and forwards rocking of the upper body. This is transferred down your spine to your seat where it irritates and can confuse your horse and certainly affects your balance for the worse.

As a sensitive, caring rider, you will obviously not wish to create a fixed, rigid and harsh contact in your horse's mouth, but I'd like you not to fall into the usual trap of moving your hands and elbows backwards and forwards with each nod of his head. This normally happens most in walk and to some extent in canter but very little in trot as the horse's head is fairly steady in that gait. The way to do it is to open and close your fingers around the reins instead. This allows your arms, elbows and hands to remain still – toned but not stiff, of course, and definitely not gripping. In this way, your upper body will not be tempted to rock back and forth, which in turn badly affects your balance.

In gallop, the horse's head makes much more marked backwards and forwards movements but it is still possible to keep your elbows fairly well in place by not only opening and closing your fingers but also flexing your wrists back and forth with the movement. In a truly fast gallop, of course, you will need to move your arms more backwards and forwards, the best way being to let the horse take as much rein as he needs as he stretches out (your hands passively following his mouth) and for you to take it gently back as he comes back, in each stride. Don't flap your elbows; keep them in and controlled as much as possible.

YOUR HEAD AND EYES

Hold your head exactly on the top of your neck, not tilted or held sideways, forwards or downwards. (This latter was the great idiosyncrasy of Nuño Oliveira, see p.8. He said that everybody was entitled to one fault and that this was his. Despite it, he was still probably the greatest classical rider of the 20th century. However, hardly any of the rest of us have so much talent that we may consciously allow ourselves a fault so we have to try to correct all our faults as best we can.) It is surprising how sensitive many horses are to your head position so you need to control it like any other part of your body. For the most part, your face should be directed between your horse's ears although sometimes looking where you want to go with only your eyes does not have the desired effect; then a subtle turn of the head in the required direction does the trick.

With your head slightly pushed up on the top of your neck or, as some prefer to think of it, pulled up on a rope from the top, and the back of your neck pressed gently back a little, look ahead and, again, get the feel of this position by just sitting still, stretching up from the waist, dropping down from the waist, elbows back in place on your hips, thumbs on top of your hands and your legs still hanging down, feeling for your seat bones.

TAKING UP YOUR STIRRUPS

When you are feeling more familiar with this position, take up your stirrups, ideally by just raising your toe, not your heel or knee, and getting a friend to put the stirrup under the ball of your foot.

When you are sitting relaxed, properly and happily, with your feet in the stirrups, looking forwards, your friend looking at you from the side should be able to imagine a vertical line dropping down through your ear, shoulder, elbow/hip and ankle bone. You are now in a perfectly balanced position, in the deepest part of your saddle. Again, hold this for a minute or so, mentally relaxing and going through the points again in your mind. If possible, it may help to get your friend to read them to you.

Before you ask your horse to move, remember that you are enjoying this! It is not a test or exam. Smile and your horse will relax. Stroke him on the lower neck/wither area which horses like, and speak to him. He's sure to wonder when work is going to start.

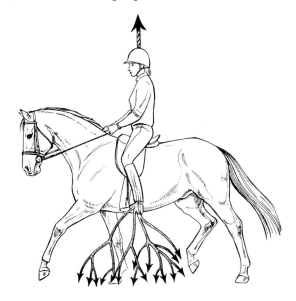

It really helps you to deepen your seat and stabilize your legs if you imagine your feet rooted firmly into the ground as you ride. To help the upward-stretching action of your upper body, too, imagine there is a rope gently pulling upwards from the top of your head

How to move with your horse

These may well be new techniques to you so give yourself time to get used to them. Do not give up if you fail a few times and do not pressure yourself (which causes tension) or rush yourself (you have no deadline, after all).

MOVING OFF

Take your feet out of the stirrups again, check your position – held upper body, relaxed lower body – and give your horse an inward, not backward, squeeze or gentle pinch with the inside of your calves, plus the command 'walk on' or whatever he obeys, and open your fingers to allow him to move. Do not keep your legs on. This is a common fault that ultimately makes for 'dead' sides. We are aiming for lightness and effortlessness, remember. Give the aid on and off within a second. A cooperative and reasonably well-schooled horse will move off to those aids. If he doesn't, try again a little stronger and get your friend to stand at his hip and click her tongue or touch him gently with a whip on his quarters or thigh. The absolute instant he moves stop the aid. He will understand, then, that he has done the right thing. If you keep your legs on he will not know (other than perhaps from habit) whether or not he has complied as – to him – you are still asking. This is confusing and, again, does not make for instant responsiveness and lightness.

THE WALK

Horses usually begin a stride (in this case of four beats) with a hind foot. Remember what we said about that side of the back dipping when a hind foot is lifted (pp.35–37)? The leg/foot passes through the air and the back is still dipped as it has temporarily lost its support. When the foot lands, the hip and back rise again as it pushes on the ground. In order to adapt your seat's movements to your horse's movements, you need to be able to feel when the back is dipping and rising.

What to do

1. Holding your upper body erect, sitting on your seat bones and pushing them just very slightly forward, and with your seat and legs loose and your legs dangling, look ahead and see if you can feel your horse's back dipping and rising from side to side under your seat. It is easier if you close your eyes as you find that you concentrate better on what is happening to your body rather than the outside world. It is also easier if the horse moves on in an active, swinging walk so that his action is more exaggerated. You may need to give him the aid occasionally to maintain this, but be sure to let your legs

go completely loose again afterwards. Alternatively, your friend could keep him walking on.

2. In order to feel the alternate dipping and rising, and the ribcage swinging from side to side under you, you must be completely loose in the seat and legs, and you must sit up and still. What will then happen is that your seat bones will naturally move with the horse's back (and hind leg) movements because there is no stiffness to stop them doing so. As, say, the right hind comes up and forward, that side of the horse's back loses its support (from the hind leg) so will dip, and his ribcage will swing to the opposite side against your left leg. Remember the barrel-on-a-rope description (p.36). The left hind will then do the same – lift and come through the air so the left side of the back dips and the ribcage swings to the right against your right leg.

3. As each hind foot lands, the back and hip under and behind your seat will rise and your seat on that side will be pushed up and forward by it because you are loose and not stiffly preventing it. Therefore, the two sides of your seat are alternately dipping and then rising forward in synchrony with the horse's movements. This alternate

Take note

• When first learning this, many riders feel the swing of the hips and the back/ribcage and let their upper bodies tilt and swing from side to side as well. This is because they are not holding their upper bodies gently but definitely stretched up and still, and have not yet grasped the idea of the upper body belonging to the rider and the lower body to the horse. Think of the dividing point as the waist and of the movement being absorbed in this area and below, in the lower back and hips.

• Do not automatically think that your hips are too stiff. No normally conformed, healthy person has hip joints too stiff to make this slight movement. What often happens is that the rider is not really letting go of the tension in their seat and thighs, and is trying to ride without stirrups with the heels pushed down and the toes up because this is so often taught. Don't do it! Keep your buttocks and legs completely loose as you learn to let yourself go with the swing.

• In halt and walk, it is quite easy to keep your position because the walk has no strong, upward thrust or moment of suspension so you can concentrate on blending with the movement.

Brodie and Alice demonstrate in walk the dipping of the hips of both horse and rider in unison. Here, their left hips are dipping ...

... and here their right hips. The rider keeps her upper body straight and upright, in tone, and does not let it sway from side to side, as is so often seen. All the movement is absorbed passively in the hips and seat. This is not possible without a relaxed seat and legs

movement is like your own natural up-and-down hip movement when you walk. You could call it walking on your horse. Because you are loose and moulded to him, your hips and seat bones are moved by your horse, not by you. This clearly cannot happen if you are tense and stiff.

Once you think you are more used to the sensation of this movement, change the rein. You will find that it feels different now, but start all over again on this rein and let yourself go into the movement.

Building on the foundations

• Next, take up your stirrups. Keep your legs and seat loose while you allow yourself to go with the swing, even though the stirrups now support your legs. Relax, remember how to sit and just keep practising. You will get it, if not on your first try then fairly soon if you relax and take your time.

• Now add a little tone in your lower legs so that they don't swing about and inadvertently hit the horse, giving an unintentional aid. This is not too likely to happen in walk. Your legs should generally be in position with your ankle joint under your hip joint although, as you will read as we go on, there are times when ithe lower leg moves in order to give an aid in an appropriate position.

• Once you have achieved a fair measure of success in walk, it is time to progress to the other gaits. This is where many people's problems start because, unlike walk, there is a moment of suspension and a significant up and down movement in every other gait (sitting trot, rising trot, canter and gallop, not to mention jumping).

A good position, with stirrups, at sitting trot, the movement being absorbed passively in the rider's lower back, hips and seat area

SITTING TROT

It only seems to have taken a couple of generations for the knowledge of how to do a soft, absorbing sitting trot to have become lost. I often see riders with impressive qualifications and others competing at the highest levels who clearly cannot do it. They tense up and grip with their legs in an effort to reduce the inevitable banging on the horse's back which comes with not knowing how to adapt to the movements of the poor horse. Another 'crime' they commit, because they are not absorbing the movement in the seat and lower back, is the 'nodding dog' syndrome. It can be seen everywhere – riders in sitting trot whose heads are nodding forward and back in time with the horse's rhythm. They are 'absorbing' the movement in their heads and necks where it cannot possibly benefit either themselves or, most importantly, their horses.

In trot, the horse has a moment of suspension, then lands, then comes suspension again, then landing on the other diagonal, and so on, so his spine is rising and falling continuously: this is in addition to the already familiar side to side dipping-and-rising movement of the back, and also the swing of the ribcage although this is not so obvious in trot.

Sitting trot is awful for both you and your horse if you get out of sync or do not know how to absorb the movement. This is where your lower back comes into play. Your lower back, seen from the side, curves slightly forward at and just below the waist (see p.70). You can easily hollow and flatten your back here. Try it now on the ground. Hollow your back by pushing forward at the waist and sticking your bottom out a little. Now flatten your spine by pushing the small of your back backwards. You will find, also, that the bottom of your pelvis (your seat bones) also tilts naturally backwards a little as you hollow your back and forwards as you flatten it. This is exactly the movement you need to do in sitting trot. Rather, this is the movement you have to allow your spine to make (by being relaxed in the seat and hip area) in response to your horse's back rising and falling.

This movement is known as the 'pelvic tilt' to dancers, gymnasts and anyone who practises any kind of body therapy, such as yoga or Pilates. It is exactly the same movement your horse makes when he engages his hindquarters and flexes his lumbo-sacral joint (see Gallop, p.42). The feeling you need to experience is one of taking up and letting down the movement of your horse's back with your seat and thighs.

The 'walking on your horse' idea (pp.80–81) is the other part of the sitting trot movement, or rather you are now 'running on your horse'. It is the same alternate dipping and rising forward action of the hips and seat bones combined with the hollowing and flattening of the lower back. I stress that if you keep your seat and legs loose, your aim being to keep your seat softly moulded around the saddle, and allow your seat to follow the horse's movements, he will show you what to do.

'For many people, sitting trot remains a mystery for all their life!'

The ideal horse

To learn to adapt to and absorb the horse's movements in sitting trot, you ideally need a horse with a very smooth trot that will keep on trotting steadily without much urging from you. This means that his action is quite easy to follow for a 'beginner' (in this method) and that you do not have to worry too much about keeping him going. However, whatever horse you end up using, the principles remain the same.

What to do

Keep the same basic posture as for halt and walk. You use this for canter as well. To start with, it is much easier to do it with long, loose, dangling legs, no stirrups, toes pointing naturally down and your upper body held but not forced and ever so slightly inclined back in a 'Native American trot' as seen in Western films. It is actually much easier to do this if you lean back just a little, to get you going. You have just practised hollowing and flattening your lower back on the ground. Now you are going to do it on your horse. Keep your seat and legs really loose, remember, otherwise you will bang on your horse's back.

Have in your mind that you are not really moving actively (even though you may be at first), rather that you are taking up and letting down your horse's movements, that he is moving you and doing the work for you – you are allowing your spine to move forward and back and your hips and seat bones to dip and then rise forwards in a slight rotation, to keep your seat softly in contact with the saddle rather than banging up and down on it.

Read the following five points, slowly and calmly picturing each of the movements; then read them again.

1. As your horse lands with the two feet of one diagonal on the ground, absorb the movement of the impact by slightly hollowing the small of your back (your lower back). Your tummy will come forward a little and the lower part of your pelvis (your seat bones) will go back a little. If your horse is landing on the left diagonal (left hind/right fore), your seat and hip on the left side will be pushed and rotated up and forwards and those on the right will dip down and back with the natural movement of his back (because his right hind is in the air, along with the left fore).

2. As your horse bounds up into the moment of suspension, slightly flatten your lower back, taking up the upward thrust under your seat and thighs. Your tummy will come back and the lower part of your pelvis will go forward again.

3. As your horse lands on the other diagonal (right hind and left fore), again absorb the impact by slightly hollowing the small of your back. The left side of your seat and left hip will dip (because the left hind is in the air) and your right side will rotate upward and forward.

Alice's excellent first attempt at getting the feel of the 'Native American trot' as the way to learn a soft, sitting trot. In sitting trot without stirrups, she keeps her seat and legs completely loose, letting her legs dangle down, and leans back just a little, allowing her seat to follow passively the movements of Brodie's back

4. Again, as the horse's back rises in the moment of suspension, slightly flatten your lower back to take up his back underneath you.

5. As he lands on the next diagonal, slightly hollow your back and allow the left side of your seat to dip while the right side is again rotated up and forward – and so on for as long as you want to stay in sitting trot.

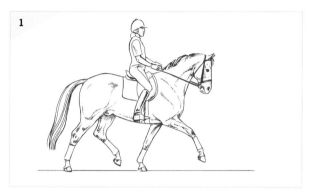

As your horse lands with the two feet of one diagonal (here the right) on the ground, absorb the impact by slightly hollowing the small of your back. Your tummy will come forward a little

As your horse bounds up into the moment of suspension, slightly flatten the small of your back, taking up the upward thrust under your seat and thighs

As your horse lands on to the other diagonal (now the left), again absorb the impact by slightly hollowing the small of your back

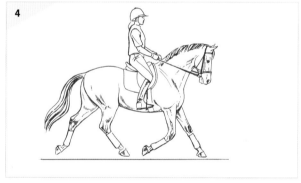

Again, as the horse's back rises in suspension, slightly flatten the small of your back to take up his back underneath you

As he lands on the next diagonal (the right again), slightly hollow your back

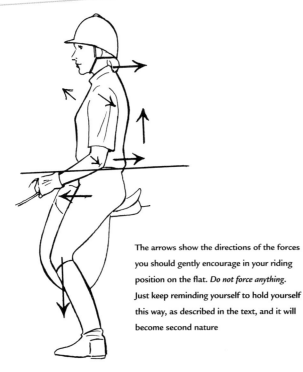

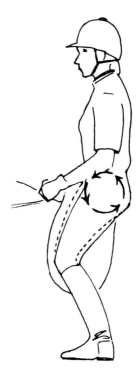

The arrows show the directions of the forces you should gently encourage in your riding position on the flat. *Do not force anything.* Just keep reminding yourself to hold yourself this way, as described in the text, and it will become second nature

Allow the movement of your horse's back to slightly move your thigh passively up and down with the pushing-off and lifting, respectively, of each hind leg. The arrows at the hip show how your hips rotate in the 'walking on your horse' movement

The same trot from behind, showing that the rider is following the horse's back with her seat, as the hips dip to the right ...

... and to the left

Take note

• Be assured that everything in sitting trot happens much more easily on the horse than thinking about it as you read. If you completely chill out and keep your upper body still, held and very slightly inclined backwards to start with, and your seat and lower legs completely loose, you really will get it with a little practice.

• If you get one or two strides and then lose it, come back to walk rather than struggling to get it right as this will cause frustration and the dreaded tension. Some people find it easier to do a low rising trot instead, then sit and try again. Much depends on the horse: some won't take kindly to repeatedly doing a very few strides of trot, then walking, then trotting again and so on.

• This technique will mean that you are not banging up and down and torturing your horse but alternately taking up and following down his back with your seat and thighs. Your horse will be amazed and comfortable, and you will feel – and be – brilliant!

A very important aspect of balance and moving in unity with your horse is that your head and shoulders stay still and on the *same level throughout the gait*. This applies to any gait with a suspension phase in it – trot, canter and gallop. Your head and shoulders will move along on a straight line, not bob up and down, because all your movement will be from the waist down and you are adapting to the movement – taking it up and following it down – with your lower back and, when you have your stirrups, with your hip, knee and ankle joints which flex and open to accommodate the rise and fall of the horse's trunk (see also p.117).

No, not *passage* but an easy, balanced sitting trot, with Sky in his bitless bridle. Note the freely swinging back and tail, indicating comfort and relaxation

A forward-going rising trot, in the rise phase. The rider is rising neatly forward and as little as possible

RISING TROT

I'm not certain how the rising trot came about. The early riding literature that I have read does not mention it. Dési Lorent (p.8) used to say it was invented by the British but that the British were the only ones who didn't know how to do it. It seems to have had something to do with the development of fox hunting as a major sport in Britain, which led to much cross-country riding and jumping, whereas on the continent of Europe, more emphasis was still placed on military and artistic schools of riding. In earlier centuries, when the roads could not easily take horse-drawn vehicles, horses ridden for transport normally used lateral gaits such as the amble to carry their riders smoothly and quickly for long distances. As roads

In the sit phase, the rider has sat down gently and her upper body position (shoulders just over her knees) has not changed throughout the movement. Her leg, similarly, has remained stable and in place

improved and vehicles became more common, such gaits went out of fashion.

The main trick to doing a good rising trot is to move as little as possible, just easing the seat forwards, instead of consciously rising, and sitting gently down, not backwards. It is a 'forward-sit' movement, not an 'up-down' one. Once your horse is trotting, this is quite easy to do as his impetus will bring your hips forward and all you have to do is sit downwards again, gently. It also helps to think of taking some weight down the insides of your thighs, too, instead of bearing it all on the stirrups as this helps to stabilize your legs and keep you closer to your horse. Later in this section, we'll talk about rising trot without stirrups.

What to do

1. Your position for rising trot is to have your back straight, bending forward a little from the hips, not the waist, with your shoulders just above your knees, and still, with the feeling of shoulders back and down and chest raised a little. Hunching forward reduces the stability of your upper body whereas staying too upright makes it more difficult to go with the forward movement. Think of it as all your movement being in your seat, and not much there, either.

2.Throughout the gait, keep your legs softly and loosely dropped down your horse's sides, both on the 'forward' and the 'sit'. Hold your legs in tone, still and, if you tend to flap them about, think of pointing towards your horse's hocks with your heels. An important factor is to really let your ankles relax so that weight drops out and down through your heels. It is a very common fault to keep the ankle stiff and to push up with the legs.

3. In a good walk, give your horse an inward on-off squeeze or pinch with the inside of your calves and maybe use whatever word you usually use to ask him to trot. In the position described and holding your upper body firm but not stiff, as he trots just push your hips forward on one diagonal and sit downwards on the other, making as little movement as possible, in practice letting your horse move you forward. As you sit, just slightly tuck your bottom under a little which will reduce your movement even more and neaten up your position. This is not because it looks better but because it keeps your movement more 'together' and controlled. Remember to drop your legs lightly and in a relaxed way on each beat but keep them toned and controlled, close to your horse without gripping

RISING TROT WITHOUT STIRRUPS

Why on earth would anyone want to do rising trot without stirrups? It sounds impossible, anyway, and seems pointless. However, if you have mastered rising trot as already described it is quite easy, and it is useful for developing more control of your own body and to give the horse's back and mind a break while you are learning sitting trot (which is easiest done without stirrups). If you are struggling a little with sitting trot, don't fight it: just go into rising trot for a few strides and try again. If you are without stirrups, the way to do it is this: just let your legs drop around your horse and assume the rising trot position. Take your weight down the insides of your thighs, and push your seat bones and pubic bone forward as you 'rise' (allowing your horse to take you forwards and up), then sit gently down again, and so on. That's all there is to it. Don't tense up, hunch forward or grip with your knees, which will stiffen your legs and seat, weaken your position and create more difficulties. Don't force your heels down or your toes up as if you had stirrups: again, this just contributes to stiffness. You may need to 'hold' your legs in position a little more than when you have stirrups, but this does not amount to actually gripping. Just do a few steps at a time to become proficient, then you can use it when you need it.

In sitting trot, imagine a ceiling immediately above your head. You cannot let your head bob up and down because you will hit the ceiling. All your horse's movement must be absorbed in the small of your back and your hips, and by using the pelvic tilt, described earlier. The parallel lines indicate the vertical movement of the horse's body, which the rider should absorb with her joints

In a fast canter or cross-country seat, most of the movement is absorbed by means of your hip and knee joints slightly opening and closing as your horse's trunk moves up and down. In this way, your head can stay quite still, running along just under the ceiling. Watch top racing jockeys and note how still their heads remain in gallop

In a slower canter, again the pelvic tilt, the opening and closing of your hip joints and the slight hollowing and flattening of the small of your back enable you to move fluidly with your horse and keep your head level under that ceiling

91

CANTER

I have already explained that in canter the leading leg affects the horse's back – say, the horse is leading with his right leg, then the right side of his back is carried slightly in front of the left side (see pp.40–41). In order to sit in harmony with the horse in canter, therefore, and ensure that the horse is comfortable in his back and gait, the rider must place the seat bone on the leading leg side slightly in front of the other seat bone. And not only the seat bone but the shoulder, too, so that the whole of that side of her body is 'leading', like the horse's back. This positioning of the seat and upper body in canter applies on both straight lines and on bends and circles. If you are in right canter whether on a straight line, going round a bend or riding a circle, you put the inside (right) seat bone and shoulder slightly forward. If you are in left canter, likewise, you put the inside (left) seat bone and shoulder slightly forward.

'This slight but greatly significant positioning of the rider's seat and upper body in canter has a magical effect on the horse.'

Not only is the horse comfortable but also he feels that the rider is really going with him and on the same wavelength. It makes the canter much easier for him under weight and acts as an instruction or reassurance to him to stay in canter. This is an old classical feature of riding canter that seems, like so many other things, to have been largely lost over the last few decades. It is discussed more in chapter 8, The aiding system, pp.120–143.

In addition to sitting so that your seat blends with your horse's back position, you also have to contend once again with the up and down movement of the horse's back in canter. This time, it feels like a forward-and-backward rocking movement (although it is not a true rocking movement), and is three-time, with a moment of suspension after the third beat. It is a rider's natural inclination to counteract any similar movements by making opposite movements with their upper body. Watch any child on a rocking horse. As the front end of the horse rocks upwards her upper body swings forwards and as it rocks down again her upper body swings back. This is no way to ride canter on a real horse but many riders do it instinctively, disturbing their horse's balance as they do so.

What you need to do is keep your upper body ramrod straight up (remember the rope pulling you up from the top of your head) and, as usual, held there in muscular tone

This is a good, balanced seat for a fast canter. The rider leans forward slightly from the hips, not the waist, with a flat back, and you could draw a straight line from her shoulder, through her knee to her toe

but not stiff. You can then allow the horse to rock away underneath your seat, once more taking up and letting down his movements by hollowing and flattening the small of your back, but also by allowing your hip joints to open and close as your thighs go up and down a little with the horse's trunk.

What to do

Imagine that the horse is in left canter and you are sitting upright with your left seat bone and shoulder slightly forward of your right seat bone and shoulder.

1. The horse starts a stride with his right hind: as it lands (on the first beat of canter) the front part of his body is up. You allow the small of your back to flatten, to take up the movement under your seat and, letting your legs drop down into your stirrups, allow your hip joints to close slightly as the horse's body moves your thighs upwards a little. This is a passive movement on your part. If you sit up and remain relaxed in your seat and legs, it will happen.

2. As the left hind and right fore land on the second beat, the horse's body levels out. Your lower back starts to hollow slightly, and you let your legs drop and your hip joints open. Sit upright, remember.

3. On the third beat – the left (leading) fore landing – the hindquarters rise. Your back continues to hollow a little more and your hip joints to open, until the left fore leaves the ground.

Don't be at cross-purposes with your horse

It is often taught that you should bring your outside shoulder round a turn 'to help the horse', and sometimes, that your hips should align with the horse's hips and your shoulders with the horse's shoulders. This teaching is based on the old, misconceived idea that on a turn the horse's spine should bend or flex on a perfect arc round the curve, following the line of the curve, causing the horse's inside hip and shoulder to be close together and the outside ones further apart. We have known for many years that this cannot and does not happen – partly because the horse's spine (apart from the neck and tail) is only slightly flexible (p.53).

If you do ride in that way, your inside seat bone and hip will be forward, but your outside shoulder – instead of the inside one – will be forward, too. This means that, in effect, you are twisted and riding at cross-purposes with your horse's natural position, which is uncomfortable for you and him. It can cause difficulties in obtaining correct, or any, canter strike-offs, poor quality of movement in canter, breaks in gait back down to trot because the horse finds it uncomfortable or difficult to maintain canter and, almost certainly, at least a moderate level of anxiety and frustration in the horse – and often in the rider, too, because of all the problems and discomfort.

Although your shoulder is not in direct contact with your horse, he can sense its position because it affects the balance and flow of forces in your upper body. If it is positioned like this it will be disturbing them and transmitting an awkward feel to him. As they do with plenty of other poor riding techniques, many horses tolerate this, bite the bullet and get on with it, but how much easier, more enjoyable and more logical for both horse and rider to use a technique which actually accords with how the horse's body works and which is more comfortable for the rider, too.

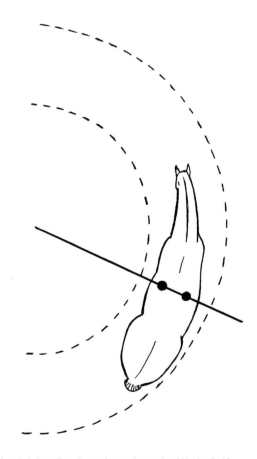

On a bend or circle in walk and trot, the seat bones should be level with each other and along the radius of the circle with the shoulders directly above them. Picture this, and you will not be in doubt about how to position yourself

4. The horse is now in the moment of suspension and his body is again horizontal as it moves through the air with the hooves gathered together underneath the belly. Your lower back is less hollowed and your hip joints close a little.

5. As the right hind comes forward and lands, the stride sequence starts again. The front part of the trunk rises … and you are back to point 1.

The whole movement is a smooth cycle of alternating lower back movements and opening and closing of the hip joints – with, of course, your inside seat bone placed just that little bit forward. The movements your back and hips make are determined by how much the horse moves under you. They may be very slight on a smooth-moving horse or you may find yourself moving more on a big-moving one. Once you get the hang of this movement, it is important to consider the movements as passive – you let your body make them in response to the horse's movements. This is truly riding as one with your horse.

To go in a straight line, this rider is riding with her seat bones level and her shoulders directly above them

To turn left, or in left canter, she moves her left seat bone forward a little with her left shoulder directly above it. She is, therefore, not twisted but riding in a way which clearly and naturally communicates with her horse and accords with his own movements

GALLOP

The gallop is a smooth progression (we hope!) from canter. There is no definite transition, as such, between canter and gallop. From the point of view of your position and seat, however, you'll find it very difficult and uncomfortable to sit the way you sit for walk, trot and canter, making the exact same movements, once you are in gallop. The old paintings of jockeys bolt upright and with long stirrups look comical now, but that is how they used to sit until the 'forward seat' gradually developed in the 19th and early 20th centuries.

The comfortable and balanced way to sit in gallop is actually a stance because your seat is barely in the saddle. You will need your stirrups a few holes shorter. Bring your upper body forward from the hip joints, not the waist, so that your shoulders are about over your knees. It is important that you keep your back flat and not rounded or hunched forward. The feel is still one of back flat, shoulders back and down and chest raised a little. Maintain this posture by slightly bracing or contracting the muscles of your upper body, particularly down your back, so that they are in 'tone' (p.15).

What to do

Aim to keep your head and shoulders still, running along a straight, horizontal line, as in the other gaits, letting the movement be absorbed in your lower body, as usual. Even in this gait, your upper arm should be dropped vertically downwards and your lower leg should lie alongside your vertical stirrup leather. This is not being picky or unrealistic – it really helps to preserve your balance (which is crucial to your security and safety) and so acts as a non-interference technique for your horse, enabling him to use himself to best effect.

'The comfortable and balanced way to 'sit' in gallop is actually a stance because your seat is barely in the saddle.'

Racehorses and work riders on the gallops. This kind of riding depends largely on balance because the stirrups need to be so short. The best work riders and jockeys have the knack of keeping their heads still and letting the movement be absorbed by their flexing hip, knee and ankle joints

In gallop, you adapt to your horse's up-and-down movement by closing and opening, respectively, your hip, knee and ankle joints. Drop your legs down your horse's sides, taking some weight down the inside of your thighs and allowing the rest to drop down through your heel. You must keep your joints flexible so that they can passively open and close according to how much the horse lifts and drops his trunk.

Imagine your horse is in a hand-gallop or three-quarter speed gallop with his right fore leading. Remember, the

gallop is a four-beat gait so his footfall will be left hind, right hind, left fore, right (leading) fore.

1. As his left hind impacts with the ground, the front part of his trunk will rise and your joints will be closed a little by the movement.

2. As his right hind and left fore legs land, his body is stretched out and more or less horizontal so your joints will open a little.

3. As his right (leading) fore lands, his hindquarters and the rear part of his back rise and your joints open a little more.

4. As his right fore lifts and he is in suspension, his trunk is once more horizontal and your joints start to close.

5. Then his left hind impacts and you are back to point 1.

As with the other descriptions of moving in each gait, this is much quicker to do than to read – especially in gallop!

JUMPING

Your body movements when jumping are very similar to those of gallop – most of the movement is absorbed by your joints. You need the same forward-inclined upper body but, for safety and balance, it is important that you do not get too far forward. Most people who fall off when galloping and jumping do so forwards, over the horse's head or shoulder. Maintaining the still, toned, controlled and superbly balanced position described for gallop will help prevent this and keep you safer.

The position for jumping changes over the years but the one I teach has stood the test of time as far as safety, balance, control and effectiveness is concerned. It enables you to sit as still as possible, give the horse maximum freedom to make his effort, interfere as little as possible with his crucial balance in this potentially dangerous part of riding and, in fact, actually help him.

Your watchwords for jumping are STILL, QUIET and BALANCED – and I might add, no clutter on your horse. If a horse needs harsh or complicated bits or nosebands or other coercive gadgets, he is not ready to be jumping – his schooling and riding need more work.

What to do

As your horse approaches his fence, adopt your position to that described for gallop on pp.96–97.

1. As he approaches and prepares for take off, his head and neck need absolute freedom otherwise, because of the way his eyes work, he cannot see the fence! This does not mean that you have a flapping rein but a very light passive contact so that he does not have to fight for his head to see what he has to tackle. Many refusals and run-outs are caused by this, and quite understandably so.

2. As he lifts his forehand, head and neck in take-off, you will feel them come back towards you a little. At this point, do not haul yourself up by the reins, throw or lurch yourself forwards or throw your hands up his neck towards his ears. Instead, fold down by allowing your hip and knee joints to be closed by the horse's upward movement. Keep your hands still. Most certainly do not snatch them back to support your body, as so very often seen, because the horse is, within a fraction of a second, going to need to stretch out his head and neck and a jab in the mouth will discourage or prevent him from doing this.

3. As the horse's hind feet leave the ground, he is in the flight phase. Keep folded down, as though you are trying to touch the crest of his neck with your breastbone and let your hands and arms be carried forward and down

Introducing Pauline Finch's six-year-old but rather green piebald, Nawato Haiatha (Sky), ridden by his trainer, Jo Birkbeck, BHSII. In this sequence, Jo is having only her second session using the style of jumping I teach. The method produces a minimalist, balanced and free method of jumping which was common years ago. Jo is in a light/half seat approaching a small double, her shoulders just above her knees, her back flat, her seat just out of the saddle, her lower leg well down and the stirrup leather vertical, and her hands and forearms in the classic, straight line elbow-hand-horse's mouth position

The flight phase and Jo continues to allow Sky maximum freedom. This is often the point when riders have their hands on the horse's neck, leaning on it for balance because they lack an independent seat and so completely restricting his movement. When she is totally familiar with this method Jo will be able to maintain the lightest contact

towards the horse's mouth as he stretches his head and neck down, performing his bascule. Keep the classic straight line, elbow-hand-horse's mouth.

4. As he comes down towards the landing phase, keep your seat off his back and slightly up out of the saddle so as not to interfere with his hindquarters and legs, and allow your joints to open a little as you raise your upper body again back into the gallop position.

Just taking off and the horse slightly raises his head as his forehand comes up. This is the point at which many riders, wrongly, pull back with their hands to haul their upper bodies forward, pulling on the mouth, restricting the horse's head and neck and seriously hampering his balance and, therefore, his jumping effort and ability to do his best

Jo's upper body is folded down (as though trying to touch the crest of Sky's neck with her breastbone), if a little too far forward. Her hands follow Sky's mouth, keeping the correct hand position which allows Sky as much freedom of his head and neck as he wants over this little cross-pole. The lack of contact is far better than keeping the head and neck held in by gripping the reins and pressing the hands on the horse's neck to aid the rider's security

The landing phase. Jo retains her light seat and good hand and arm position. Her basic position has hardly changed throughout the jump

She stays up out of the saddle so as not to bang Sky on the back with her seat, and maintains the free rein to allow Sky to regain his balance

The get-away ... Jo keeps her still half-seat

Jo is sitting still and in the same position, as Sky is on his way to the next element of this double

5. On landing, keep the gallop position with your toned upper body, to avoid being pulled forwards on landing. The horse will be raising his head and neck as he is about to land and hopefully will make a smooth get-away – the final phase.

6. As he resumes his canter stride – the get-away – maintain your gallop position to keep his hindquarters free until he is well and truly on the flat again. The modern technique is to sit fairly upright between fences but a controlled, balanced gallop position throughout your track is fine also.

Take note

· Reread point 3 where I talk about the downward inclination of the hands, pointing towards the horse's mouth during the jump. This is much more logical and more effective than having the hands thrust up towards the horse's ears (creating an upside-down V-shape with the hands at the top), which is so commonly seen. Maybe riders do this in the belief that they are 'lifting' the horse over the fence, but, of course, it is quite impossible to lift a horse over a fence by riding him! What this hand position actually does is restrict the horse's head and neck at the very moment when he needs absolute freedom to stretch them out and down as much as demanded by the height and spread of the fence. The shortest route between two points is a straight line so, by keeping

The approach to the second element of the double, a small spread. Note that you could draw a more or less vertical line from Jo's shoulder, touching her knee and down to her toe. This is an excellent approach position: Jo is not in front of the movement but will not be 'left behind' either

Sky is about to take off and Jo keeps her position, refraining from pulling herself forward with her hands because she has such good balance

Jo's excellent balance, secure position and 'giving' hand technique allow her to really go with Sky, who flies through the air with the greatest of ease, enjoying the freedom of a rider who lets him jump properly and is able to go with him without banging him on the back or jabbing him painfully in the mouth

Jo could be a little more up out of the saddle but does not need the reins to regain her balance, giving Sky his head to enable him to regain his own balance as he starts his landing

the straight elbow-hand-horse's mouth line, you are giving your horse maximum help to get the pair of you over the fence. Over a big fence, it may be necessary for you to slip your reins (let them run through your fingers) for as much as the horse needs to take.

· A point I also stressed when talking about galloping is the need to keep your lower leg down so that your stirrup leather remains vertical. This is the only way you will stay in the best balance possible. Tilting the legs backwards from the knee, usually with toes down, weakens your seat. Sticking your legs forwards sends your seat back to the cantle, unless you are tackling a fairly big drop fence, and encourages you to brace on the horse's mouth – a heinous crime in any humane, effective method of riding but particularly in jumping when freedom of the head and neck are absolute necessities.

· Finally is the instruction to fold down by closing your joints, concertina-like, rather than throwing yourself forwards. Folding down maintains a secure, in-balance position on the horse's back. There will be an imaginary straight, vertical line from your shoulder, through your knee and touching your toe, to the ground. Surprisingly enough, I have analysed a good deal of footage and many photographs of classical jumping riders and found that this is almost always the case, even over big fences. Today, few trainers seem to teach this but some riders still do it, perhaps partly because it comes naturally.

The take-off, and Jo folds down and keeps her hands low with a free rein to allow Sky the confidence to stretch out

He pings over this with great trust and enjoyment as Jo goes with him, folded down, lower leg always well down with a vertical stirrup leather and hands going down and forwards to follow Sky's mouth

The pair is still in balanced freedom here but ...

... Jo is a little in front of the movement a split second later as Sky gets away. Nobody's perfect!

SIT STILL AND GIVE YOUR HORSE HIS HEAD

The more you move when your horse jumps, the more you put him off. These drawings support the accompanying photographs: an independent seat allows the rider to maintain a light, balanced seat, with the shoulders just above the knees, and to fold *down* from the hips, with the hands following the horse's mouth, ideally keeping a light contact.

In take-off, do not pull yourself forward with your hands – give your horse his head

Fold down from the hips; don't throw your body forwards or your hands up

In flight, fold right down, again *not* forward, and follow down and forward to his mouth with your hands

Stay off his back in landing and do not use your hands to keep your balance

Still off his back as he gets away, keep giving him his head to enable him to balance both himself and you

'I have been using this method of jumping in my own schooling and teaching and I find that horses do jump more freely and enthusiastically ridden this way.'
Jo Birkbeck, BHSII

The feel of a correct ride

The sensation of riding a horse that is going correctly, from the back end, light to legs and hands, willing and cooperative, and ideally enthusiastic, is one you never forget. This way of going involves the vertebral bow, the ring of muscles and engagement of the hindquarters (see p.56).

The vertebral bow, with the spine held slightly arched under the rider's seat, is necessary for the horse to carry weight safely and without undue stress to his spine. An arched bridge is a strong structure and so is an arched spine. Of course, in movement the spine will still undulate slightly longitudinally (up and down) but the posture is maintained most of the time in a schooled horse, although the rider may need to ask for it. The ring of muscles is used to bring about and maintain that posture and, when it is in place the hindquarters are engaged by flexion of the lumbo-sacral joint at the croup, the pelvis being tucked slightly forward (like us tucking our bottom under a little) and the hind legs, because they are joined to the pelvis at the hip joints, also being enabled to reach further forward under the horse's belly, and asked to carry more weight as the forehand lightens.

Without the posture described, no horse will or can give that unforgettable sensation of a correct ride. A few horses do it naturally but most have to be schooled, developed and asked for it. Once they are shown how to do it, most horses, again, are willing to do it and obviously enjoy the sensations they feel in their own bodies, not to mention the freedom of working in this strong, effective way under a sensitive, balanced rider who asks questions and then allows the horse answer them without constant interruption.

I hope that, somehow, somewhere, you will be able to ride a schoolmaster (p.18) that will give you the feeling of a correct ride: you only need to feel it well and truly once for it to become ingrained on your memory and you will know for ever more what to aim at with every horse you ride. Although all horses feel different, the main impression of onward and upward impulsion is the same. Although the horse's body is, obviously, moving in its natural way underneath you, the over-riding feeling you get on his back is of being pushed and lifted from behind up and forwards by a force much stronger than you are – sort of 'riding along on the crest of a wave'. At the same time, the horse's forehand appears to lift up into your hands and all you have to do is sit still and direct it. How different from the 'grinding into the ground' feeling of a horse on his forehand or even the level, rocking-horse canter of a balanced but not impulsive horse!

A correct ride, then, is balanced, strong and stable, light to leg and hand and, ultimately, sensitive to your thoughts. There is plenty of impetus or impulsion, but no excessive speed; speed is not impulsion – it is just fast forward movement, often without good balance. Horses going that way try to steady themselves on the bit, which makes them heavy in the hand and dull in the mouth.

Use your imagination and get these descriptions into your psyche. If you experience a downward, hard, sinking, leaning or pulling feeling from your horse, with little or no response to your weight, rein, leg or even voice, if you do not feel both spiritually and physically uplifted when you are riding and if your horse in general feels badly balanced, uncooperative and no pleasure to ride, he is giving you the opposite of a correct ride. This may be because of his previous schooling and riding, or it may be because you are using the only techniques you know or have been taught and your horse does not like them, or they simply are not the most natural or effective. Don't blame yourself. Although the way he goes is at least partly because of the techniques you are using, it is not your fault if you do not know any different. Being prepared to learn to be really with your horse and moving as one close unit is the major part of this method and the following chapter gives some ideas to help you in this.

'You only need to feel a correct ride once for it to become ingrained on your memory for ever more.'

This horse and rider are moving well together, looking really 'at one'

6

Let it happen

One of the first things new clients say to me when I am teaching them this system is: 'Oh, I'm really stiff and I don't have good coordination. I don't think I'll be able to do that.' This way of riding does not require any physical abilities beyond those most human bodies possess. Compared to many other sports, riding is not particularly athletic. Most people have enough movement in their joints and loose enough soft tissues to enable them to ride in the way I describe easily enough. The main problem is often that this technique uses different principles and a different aiding system from that which many people have been taught, and – this is the difficulty – they often do not want to make the mental effort to change their ways and replace old habits with new ones. However, it is also true to say that some people are blocked from improving not because they are physically stiff as such but because they are psychologically tense. Remember, tension creates stiff muscles and those create stiff bodies (pp.14–15), so it must be addressed if any progress is to be made. Of course, you cannot change your innate temperament but there are various things you can do to learn to relax and chill out on or off your horse.

'This way of riding does not require any physical abilities beyond those most human bodies possess.'

NO EXCUSES

Attitude and self-discipline are everything in many pursuits, not least self-improvement, which is what this method of riding is. I feel that if people don't want to work at making an improving change for their own sakes, they do at least owe it to their horses.

Age, also, has nothing to do with it. There is no such thing as 'I am too old to change my ways now'. People can learn at any age. An open, enquiring, absorbing mind is the way to a fulfilled and fulfilling life. Some people acquire university degrees in their 70s and older. Others take up new sports and physical pursuits often for the first time after they retire. There are no excuses!

Conversely, children can learn this method easily, too. Just because some currently pull and yank on their ponies' mouths, know no other leg aid than a hard kick backwards with their heels, often wearing spurs (it amazes me that children are allowed to wear them), or are whip-happy to the point of cruelty, it does not mean that, with guidance and discipline, they cannot be taught to ride well instead.

And you can't use your horse as an excuse either. Although, as I said earlier, when you are learning this method it is better to ride a well-behaved and cooperative horse that you trust, you can still make giant strides by putting these principles into practice with a horse that is not like this. I have known many badly behaved (defensive) horses transform, sometimes within minutes, once they are ridden in a way that is kind and logical to them so that they are not afraid of their rider and can understand what she wants.

'Lifelong learning is a reality.
Stagnate and die is another.'

Exercises to loosen up

These simple, basic exercises, sensibly done, are excellent for anyone who has never tried this system before and for more experienced riders who want to limber up and prepare for riding. Although they can be done at any time, they make a good warm-up before mounting. I don't see any point in doing exercises like this once you are in the saddle. It is more effective to do them on the ground.

It helps to wear loose, comfortable clothing for any exercise. In fact, this also goes for riding. Even super-stretchy fabrics for breeches and other garments can restrict you if they are just too tight. You have enough things to think about when on a horse without your clothing giving you more.

If you have any physical problems at all, do consult a doctor or physical therapist before you start doing any exercises unfamiliar to you, otherwise you could make a problem worse or create another one. The first two exercises were explained earlier, on pp.20–21 because they are useful for releasing tension and calming you.

HEAD ROLL

Starting from the top, gently roll your head around both ways a few times, concentrating on relaxing your tissues and only taking things as far as is comfortable. This means pushing a bit but not hurting yourself. Forget 'no pain, no gain', which is a rubbish and dangerous statement. Pain usually means injury.

SHOULDERS

Next lift and roll your shoulders up and back and roll them around a few times, pushing them to their limits without hurting yourself. Then lift and circle both arms both ways three or four times.

HANDS

Clench and stretch your hands a few times before giving them a shake with loose wrists. This exercise relieves tension up through your arms to your shoulders as well as ensuring that your hands will be flexible on the reins to communicate gently with your horse.

Stretch your fingers and hands ...

... clench them into tight fists ...

... shake your hands and wrists ...

Stretch your fingers out again ...

... and rotate your wrists to loosen them up ...

... really move them around to ensure a sensitive, 'feeling' contact with your horse's mouth

HIPS TO ANKLES

Lift your legs sideways, straight, as high as is comfortable, without tilting your upper body in the opposite direction. Do this with both legs three or four times to gently stretch the tissues in your groin area sideways, which will help you to drape your seat and legs around your horse. Circle your ankles both ways several times and then stand with the balls of your feet on a step and let your weight drop down through your heels. Do not bounce on the step as this can cause over-stretching of tissues and injury. Just loosen your ankle joints so that they can flex fully and 'hang' there. Then raise yourself up and repeat the drop, doing this a few times.

BACK

Back exercises are really the province of specialists as back problems vary in nature: if you have back trouble, you will need to do exercises prescribed specifically for you. However, you can try practising the pelvic tilt movement. Stand up perfectly straight, then hollow the small of your back and push your bottom back a bit, then flatten your back and push your seat bones and pubic bone forwards a little, then back again, and so on. Make this a smooth, relaxed movement with no jerking.

Rotate your ankles both ways to loosen them up, as stiff ankles really have a bad effect on your relaxation and application of the aids

See if you can lift your legs horizontally to the side – excellent for hip joint and general groin suppleness. Alice is obviously not only supple but well-balanced, as she holds these poses for our photographer

Carefully swinging your legs straight forward and back works your hip joints and improves your balance generally

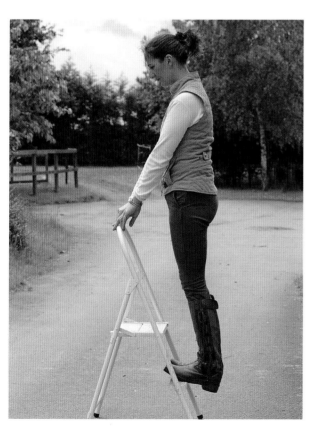

Stand on a step or step ladder making sure you are in good balance, with your toes on the step and your heels free. Drop your heels down gently to give the backs of your legs and your ankles a good stretch, then move onto tiptoes to loosen up your toes and ankles. Don't be tempted to bounce as you might overstretch the tissues

Getting serious

Suppling or loosening up is essential to good riding and ease of movement and the stretches described on pp.107–109 are a good, comprehensive start but, if you are so inclined, it is a good plan to take things further under a trained teacher. Contact a personal trainer or the trainer at your local gym to see if they can give you just one or two sessions (unless you get hooked, of course) showing you suitable exercises for your bodily condition and the sport of riding.

There are several bodywork practices that are really beneficial for anyone, and many have a mind and spirit aspect as well as a physical one. Three accessible ones – with classes in most localities – are yoga, Pilates and the Alexander Technique. There are also many books, videos and DVDs on these and other techniques, including Feldenkrais, but it would be a good plan to at least start off with formal classes or private lessons.

Yoga

The purpose of yoga is to join together the body, mind and spirit. There are several different kinds of yoga but all of them use natural movements promoted from within the body and, as such, are not forceful. However, they do stretch you – in body, mind and spirit. Yoga is brilliant for creating a loose and amazingly flexible body. Do not be put off by some of the amazing postures you may see illustrated in books and magazines. The object is not to achieve these postures but to do what is within your reach. The correct practice of yoga maintains or creates a more youthful, supple and healthy body, improving wellbeing, self-esteem and general health.

Pilates

Pilates is often used with yoga and, although it certainly stretches you, it is also a strengthening modality. Your muscles and tissues are lengthened and strengthened – no chance of becoming muscle-bound with Pilates – and your mind is trained to concentrate and to focus, and so becomes settled and controlled. Focusing on the link between the mind and body, it teaches posture among many other things, which all add up to wellbeing, raised spirits and self-confidence.

Alexander Technique

This also aims to improve your health through improving your posture. It enables your body to work in a relaxed, efficient and natural way, promoting harmony of body and mind and helping to improve many medical conditions. Because it enhances physical and emotional health, it brings about resistance to stress. It complements yoga and Pilates perfectly.

Other complementary activities

I have noticed that the people to whom it is easiest to teach riding are those who (now or in the past) practise dancing (especially classical ballet and ballroom dancing), gymnastics and skating, also skateboarding and skiing. I imagine that surfers will also grasp riding quite easily.

Classical ballet is founded on both stretching and strengthening movements, and posture, balance and bearing are critical to success. Ballroom dancing, done properly and well, also demands good posture and an independence of both the upper and lower body. The lady will learn beyond doubt how uncomfortable and difficult it is to dance well with a man who does not hold her supportively but sensitively and/or who does not lead. This is identical to the situation of horse and rider, but in this case the horse is the lady and the rider is the man. Gymnastics teaches strength, suppleness and consummate physical control and mental concentration, as does skating. You may be surprised to see skateboarding and skiing mentioned. However, think about it. To do both well you must be able to take up and let down movement created by uneven ground beneath your feet. These sports really teach you to keep your head and shoulders on a straight line, your upper body independent of your lower body, and to open and close the hip, knee and ankle joints by the exact amount needed, making adjustments according to the ground, which can be translated to mean the horse's movements under you.

All these activities require and develop coordination, good posture, mental control of the upper body and the ability to accommodate changing movements with your seat/hips and legs. Perhaps people who want to do well at them should learn to ride too.

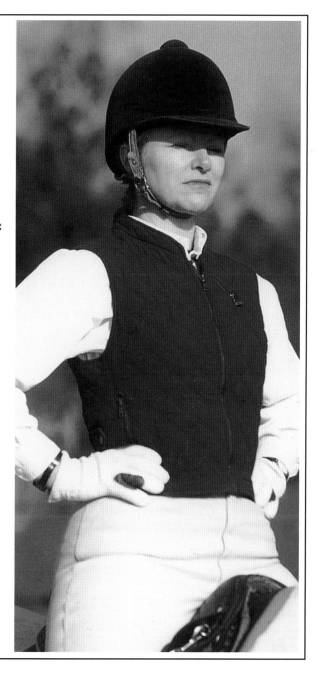

7

Mind power

The main aids in this method of riding are the mind (including the spirit) and the seat (including the thighs and bodyweight). This chapter is all about how to use your mind to communicate with your horse and ask him to do things with you, and also how to use your mind and spirit to influence yourself as your own guiding force. The seat aids are covered in the next chapter, The aiding system, pp.120–143.

Mental rehearsal, visualization, day-dreaming and a vivid imagination are all excellent and perfectly relevant ways of preparing yourself for doing something spectacular, whatever that is

A well-known phrase in the field of self-improvement is 'what you think, you are'. If you think you are useless at something you will behave as though you are, with a lack of both confidence and competence, and do it poorly. If you think you are good at something, you will behave as though you are, with self-confidence and competence, and you will do it well, provided you know how to.

Another saying is 'the job makes the man'. It is often not until someone is given a particular task or job and gets into it that they realize that they are quite capable of doing it. The phrase 'You never know what you can do till you try', is also very true. The fact that someone trusts in you enough to give you the job brings self-confidence, and self-confidence breeds competence and respect.

It is exactly like this with riding. Presumably you are reading this book because you want to change and improve the way you ride, and also the way horses go for you and generally react with you. You may have any of several different emotional states about your situation. You may be downhearted because what you are doing now clearly is not working very well. You may have loads of self-confidence and an upbeat attitude but your techniques are letting down both you and the horses you ride. You may have a lovely, sensitive and expressive natural feel for horses and riding but don't know how to put it into practice to best effect, or you may not be sure that what you think and do is 'correct'.

There are many ways to achieve horsey goals. Several are effective as far as getting horses to perform movements or behave in certain ways, but many are not logical, kind or humane, and some are downright cruel. The method I describe in this book is the kindest, most logical and most effective I have come across in my whole life. I have ridden in other ways but always come back to this one because I have never found anything as good. I constantly look for improvements that are in the best interests of the horse because life is not static and I am a firm believer in lifelong learning.

So let's explore the mind power of both the rider and the horse and see what road this leads us down.

> *'If you think you are good at something, you will behave as though you are, with self-confidence and competence, and do it well.'*

Mental pictures

From years of observation, I am certain that horses communicate with each other through mental pictures. Of course they use other means as well. They are acutely perceptive of the most minute changes in body language and of changes in their environment and they watch other creatures very closely. They may also communicate using sounds that are too high-pitched for us to pick up, but which studies have revealed that they can hear.

I am sure that horses also try to communicate with *us* using mental pictures but many of them give up because most humans don't respond or don't want to have to think on this level. Many years ago, in the early years of the Equine Behaviour Study Circle's existence (it is now known as the Equine Behaviour Forum), our members' journal, *Equine Behaviour*, featured a contribution by a gentleman called Joe Royds who described the behaviour of one of his horses during the absence of her companion at a veterinary clinic for a minor operation which required a general anaesthetic.

All the time the companion was out of her sight, the mare was very agitated. Then, when the time of the operation arrived, she suddenly went very quiet and relaxed. At about the time her companion would be recovering she became agitated again. This lasted until he arrived home, when normality was resumed.

Mr Royds believed that the mare and her companion were picturing to each other their anxiety at being apart and at what was happening to the gelding, but that the general anaesthetic broke the mental line of communication between the two horses. As it wore off, the line was 'reconnected' and the horses once again communicated with each other by means of mental pictures until they were together again.

AN EXPERIMENT TO TRY

I could describe many other instances of horses thinking to each other and to other creatures including humans, but I'll offer a very practical experiment for you to try directly connected to your riding. It is a simple exercise that I ask all new clients to do to prove the point that most horses are sensitive enough to respond to the mind alone and to start encouraging the client to think differently about how to achieve what they want to do in the saddle.

Keeping your seat and legs really loose, with your horse on a free rein so that there can be no directions from the reins, pick a landmark – a tree or a marker in your school, say – and without giving any physical aids or even muscle twitches, apart from looking at the marker with your eyes (not turning your head), think hard to your horse that you want him to walk towards it. He will do so if you keep looking at it and thinking about it, and imagining the two of you walking towards it. Your line may be wobbly and your horse uncertain at first but praise from you will confirm to him that you really are talking his language!

To check that it was not a fluke, take up your normal riding attitude and ride around for a minute, then pick a different landmark and ride in the same way towards that. You can even do this with your eyes closed. For example, just walk down the centre line, staying loose, and tell your horse, mentally only, to go left or right. He may only do it slightly, being unused to this sort of communication with you but, unless he is distracted, he will go where you ask if you keep your mind clear and expect it to happen. Be sure that you are not stopping him with physical aids, body attitude or lack of belief. Just think clearly and positively.

Your horse will always pick up on what you think and on your mood and emotions. He may not always act on them but he usually will. His acute perception of emotions, 'atmosphere' and, of course, body posture is the reason that an apprehensive, nervous or frightened rider or handler is detected by a horse immediately, but so is a calm, confident, positive one. Fear may well travel down the reins, or along the leadrope, but the emotion will reach his mind first.

Thinking to your horse is a powerful way of communicating with him and will become even more so as you and he get used to each other and your new way of communicating.

CREATING YOUR FOCUS

In Eastern modalities, such as martial arts, yoga, shiatsu, t'ai chi and others, the centre of the body is regarded as being sited just below the navel inside the abdomen. You need to think from here, move from here and be from here. From a riding point of view, lower your mind from your head to your centre so that your awareness is inside your abdomen just above your seat bones. Concentrate on this area in a relaxed way and you may be amazed to feel how light your head and upper body become and how much easier it is to control your body movements. You automatically feel better balanced because your weight seems lower and is now much closer to your horse's own centre of balance, which is inside his chest about two-thirds of the way down his ribcage about a hand's breadth, or a little more, behind his elbow. This is why riding with your seat and mind is so much more effective and secure than riding with your head, hands and lower legs. The horse can feel it and so can you if you keep doing it.

I have no practical explanation for this. I only know that it works. Get into the habit of thinking with your seat and of communicating with your horse from your centre. Keep pushing your mind down to it and you will find that you use your seat, weight and thighs more instead of your hands and lower legs. This puts you closer to your horse's core, to his centre of control and balance and immediately gives you both the feeling of being much more in harmony and secure. You do have to keep reminding yourself of it to begin with but, if you keep on doing it, it will become second nature.

'Your horse will always pick up on what you think and on your mood and emotions.'

Mind power is invaluable as a vivid communication aid. At first, horses are unsure because they are not used to people using their own method of communication (my opinion, but I'm pretty confident of it), but once they get used to it it opens up a whole new dimension between you. Here, Anne, who is not even holding the reins, thinks to Lucy and visualizes them both turning left. Lucy is just starting to turn here

Visualization

The power of mental images on our physical state cannot be ignored. Here are some of my favourites for you to try.

• A mental visualization that will help you to keep your seat and thighs firmly but gently around your horse is to imagine that they are coated with Blu-Tac (Fun-Tak). You can move and so can your horse, but the pair of you cannot come apart.

• I have already mentioned the rope pulling you upwards from the top of your head, to help you maintain a good posture (p.79). Another one, which particularly helps stability, stillness and security, is to think of your feet as like the roots of a tree, firmly grounded in the earth. These two visualizations, and many others, are detailed in Sally Swift's now classic books on her Centered Riding system (see Further Reading, p.150).

• A well-known classical concept to aid straightness and accuracy of direction, which also helps you to keep your legs and arms still and gently in position, is known as 'the corridor of the aids'. This means that your reins and legs form the walls of a narrow corridor down which your horse moves. Imagine this corridor going towards wherever you want to go and ride within it: it is really helpful. Also, try imagining a narrow-gauge railway track laid on the ground to wherever you want to go, put your seat bones on it and go.

• A visualization which should help you to keep your hands still, and just an inch or so above the withers, unless you have good reason to move them, is to think of having your little fingers slotted through elastic bands fastened to the dees on your pommel. Some people find it helpful to actually do this and it is quite harmless, of course. The gait in which hands generally seem to misbehave is rising trot: as the rider's body goes up and down (in a poor rising trot) so do their hands. If you do rising trot in the way I described earlier (pp.88–90), you will find it so much easier to keep your hands level just above the withers, because your shoulders (to which your arms are attached) are not actually going up and down any more.

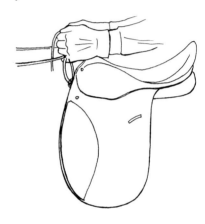

Attaching elastic bands to the pommel dees of your saddle to slot your little fingers through is a harmless but effective way of helping you to keep your hands still

Often known as the 'corridor of the aids', visualizing riding down a corridor, whether straight or on a curve, helps to concentrate your mind on straightness.

Another aid for helping you to achieve straightness is to imagine that your seatbones are running along a narrow-gauge railway track

• A wonderful visualization that gears your mind-set towards being in control of whatever you are doing on your horse is to imagine that he is strapped to your seat and that he has to follow wherever you go. You decide where you are going and you just take him with you. It never enters your head that he won't go with you because he has no choice – he's fastened to you! This is the 'firm' part of 'calm, firm and positive'. Instead of having the feeling of asking him to go somewhere, you go and just assume that he will come with you.

• Finally, here is a visualization that will really help you with keeping your head and shoulders still on a horizontal line by taking up and letting down the movements of your horse's body using your lower back and the joints of your hips, knees and ankles. Imagine that you are riding immediately under a low ceiling, which is just skimming the top of your hat. You cannot bob up and down because there is no room above your head, therefore you must absorb the up-and-down movements of your horse in your lower body, by flexing the small of your back and your leg joints. It works brilliantly.

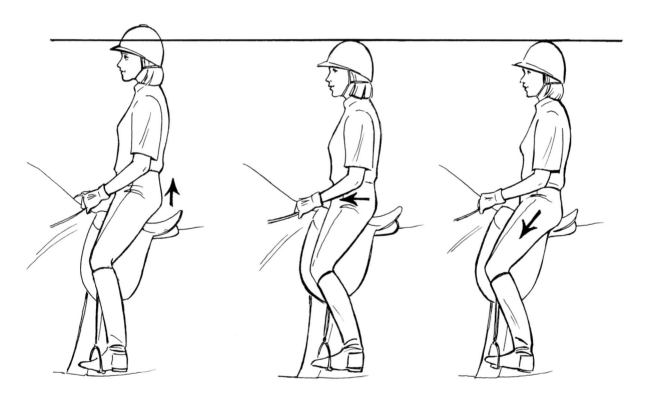

Remember the glass ceiling! Pushing yourself up and down with your legs in rising trot (above left) will certainly send your head through the imaginary ceiling! Instead, use the 'forward – sit' technique and absorb the movement in your lower body (centre and right) to enable you to keep your head below it

Mental rehearsal

This is something you can do anywhere at almost any time. Take a goal in riding you want to achieve – a particular movement you want to do or a fence you want to clear – read up on it, watch it on DVD or video as often as you like until you are sure you know all about it. Now imagine yourself and your horse doing it – including all the aids you would use and your body position – and rehearse it in your mind as often as you like. It is known that rehearsing something, then leaving it for a while – a few hours or a day or so – then rehearsing it again, and again, is the best way to get it into your mind. Your body then seems to take its cue from your mind and does what your mind tells it to do. When you get on your horse, your mind and body have already learnt what you want to do, so all you have to do is put it into practice. Your confidence rubs off on your horse and you just do it.

Remember to think it vividly to your horse so that he has a clear mental picture of it and, because you have rehearsed your body position and the aids, he gets practical direction, too. You're more than halfway there with your mental rehearsals so you just need to practise and refine it in the flesh. You might think that all this sounds a bit unlikely but, again, I know it works. Put yourself into the image, get the image inside you, know that you can do it, rehearse it, then do it.

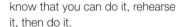

Meditation

Not advised on horseback, perhaps, but meditation is a great way of generally calming down your mind and spirit and, consequently, relaxing your body. It is not about falling asleep as you sit, cross-legged, on the floor. In fact, if you fall asleep you aren't doing it right. It is about becoming aware of your inner being (ideal for riding), of equipping yourself with a way of clearing away stresses and worries and of reaching tranquillity of body, mind and spirit. It is refreshing, utterly calming and strengthening. Once you get the knack and allow it to happen under instruction – either in person or from learning materials – you achieve the ability to manage your life in accordance with higher principles and work from a state of inner peace and enlightenment. There are umpteen books, DVDs, videos, courses and classes on meditation, almost certainly from a source near you, or by mail order. Go on – give it a whirl.

T'ai chi

T'ai chi began in China in ancient times. Its aim is to promote good posture, flexibility and balance on a physical level and, on a philosophical level, to develop perfect harmony between the ying and yang (female and male) energies of the body, promoting a smooth, unhindered flow of energy throughout the body and a feeling of 'one-ness' and deep relaxation within body, mind and spirit – the eternal trilogy.

T'ai chi consists of a series of graceful, flowing movements, performed in set patterns, which help you to control your mind and body, your breathing, your thoughts and your attitudes. From a rider's viewpoint, it softens your position yet creates superb physical control along with relaxation, promoting lack of tension. It also facilitates breathing with your horse (see right) and teaches you to communicate with him from your centre (see Creating your focus, p.114). Because your body, mind and spirit are transmitting the same thing to your horse, he understands instinctively and is enabled to cooperate with you in a true partnership. This really is an excellent way to become at one with your horse.

Sounds too good to be true? Try it – you'll find it isn't.

Breathing with your horse

A simple technique that you can do almost instantly is to breathe with and to your horse. Standing by your horse and trying to coordinate your breathing with his for a while is an excellent start. He breathes much more slowly than you, so you may need to take an in-and-out breath in time with his out or in breath.

In groundwork, because breathing can alter your posture it affects your body language and so your visual communication with your horse – a way of connecting that all horses seek. By exaggerating your breathing at appropriate times when you want to tell or ask your horse something, you can get his attention and show him what you want. Breathing in correctly expands your chest, stretches up your spine and gives you a more commanding, authoritative air; breathing out gives you a softer outline and feel, and calms the horse.

In the saddle, breathing in rhythm with his stride encourages unity between the two of you, especially if your horse is distracted or nervous. Breathing out relaxes you both and sends him on with energy and confidence, whereas breathing in lifts your upper body and can alone stop a horse that is sensitive to you. Combined with appropriate gentle but unmistakable aids, it is a powerful stopping request.

8

The aiding system

The word 'aid' means 'help', and that is what the aids should do – they are supposed to help the horse understand what we'd like him to do. They are not automatic buttons that definitely always work because the horse, no matter how good his schooling, has a mind of his own (although he does form both good and bad habits quickly). The aids work best when horse and rider are in good balance together and in a calm frame of mind. The rider needs to be clear in her positions and actions and the horse's body needs to be in such a position, and condition, that he can actually make the physical actions required. The aids often used today, and the way in which they are used, frequently do the exact opposite – they can confuse the horse, and sometimes upset him. Very often, they work against his natural inclinations, although much depends on their interpretation by the rider and instructor.

Alice carefully demonstrates on Brodie the unwanted effects of pulling back on the inside rein. Brodie clearly does not think much of it, tenses up, raises her head and neck and flattens her back – exactly the opposite of what we think we have asked for

This is a classical way of using the inside rein to invite the horse to turn and it is amazing how a horse will respond to it, even when there is no contact. Just turn your wrist like this and raise it a little

The aids

Almost without exception, the one thing new clients say to me when I explain the aids I want them to use is: 'But that's completely opposite to what I've been taught'. In many instances, this is true, but not all. The aids I use and teach are logical because they accord with the horse's natural inclinations and practices, so barely have to be taught to him. They not only inform the horse but also encourage him to comply by physically working in the language he learned as a foal from his dam and other horses and also by activating his own sense of balance. No sensible prey animal wants to lose his balance so he does his best to keep his equilibrium. These aids promote that balance and, hence, cooperation. The almost magical thing about them to riders new to the method is that horses understand them instantly.

This system uses simple, clear aids to enable the horse to follow what you are asking. Nowadays, many riders are taught to use multiple active aids at the same time, which is unnecessary and can be very confusing for the horse. It is always best to give him a little time to realize what you want, one thing at a time. Remember the maxim 'hands without legs, legs without hands' and you will start thinking along the right lines.

The main aids I use are the mind, the eyes and the seat, which includes the thighs and the rider's weight. Rein aids are used but they sometimes differ from those commonly taught. The key difference is that they *push* and *invite* the horse in the direction required, rather than pulling him around with the inside rein. This in itself helps him to retain his balance. They are positive and giving, providing reassurance and clear direction. The two reins are not used in the same way at the same time, or at precisely the same moment as the legs, because this can feel conflicting to the horse and cause anxiety.

The aiding system in a nutshell
· Uses the horse's own language
· Promotes balance and cooperation from the horse
· Uses simple, clear, individual aids

How we confuse our horses

Using more than one aid at a time or using them insensitively can make it much more difficult for a horse to understand what we want from him. To take a rather extreme but common example, think how unpleasant it must be for a horse to be 'driven up to the bit' as is so very often taught.

· The legs are driving him forwards and both hands, having a firm contact, are telling him to stop! This is compounded when the bit is too high in his mouth and, therefore, also exerting a constant pull on the corners of the lips.

· Even worse is the increasingly common technique of holding the reins tightly and short, and even pulling back on them, with the mistaken thought that this harsh, restrictive technique is 'containing the energy coming from behind'. What is actually happening is that his neck is being shortened and distorted, so:

· his breathing is being hampered by a constricted throat and a painfully tight noseband,

· the muscles of his neck, shoulders, forearms and back become tense and painful, with the end result that

· the spine sinks and the hind legs actually trail behind rather than, as the rider believes, being brought well under and forward. Many horses also appear to pull themselves along more with the forehand because they are prevented from using the hind legs effectively.

Unrelenting, hard driving from the legs (and spurring, as here) does drive the horse forward, but in a stressed, artificial and exaggerated way. Ridden and tacked up in this way he can never willingly and lightly give (flex at both poll and jaw) to the bit, stretch out and forward, balance himself and move as best he can, all of which are objectives of correctly educated riders and well-schooled horses.

The whole scenario is completely irrational. Nevertheless, photographs illustrating and apparently condoning and lauding it can be seen regularly in the horsey press.

What a miserable picture! This is often what happens when a rider tries to pull the horse in from the front with the reins and, at the same time, applies strong leg aids to 'push him up to the bit' from behind. This horse's reaction has been to try to escape the harsh bit contact by bringing his muzzle down and back. His back is sagging and hind legs trailing and he is clearly very distressed, not to mention confused

Weight and pressure

Your weight, and the way it is balanced on the horse's back, is an extremely powerful and effective aid. The usual example given of balance and weight aids is for us to imagine carrying a heavy but loose backpack: if it slips over to the left we will tend to move left, often without really thinking about it, to get back under the weight and restore a comfortable balance. So it is with the horse. If something (such as our weight and any pressures we apply to his body) suggests that forces are indicating left, the horse will quite naturally go left to keep his balance and so restore his comfort.

Let's start with the seat and leg aids as they are so important and helpful. You have read a good deal about seat bones already and the posture needed for body control and adapting to the horse's movements. Therefore, you understand the importance of sitting upright, still and centrally so as not to throw the horse off balance: the ability to sit still is greatly helped by keeping the upper body in the postures described earlier for each gait, and in moulding and dropping your seat and legs lightly down and around your horse.

Remember the 'where you put your weight your horse will go' principle. Keep your weight central from side to side as a general rule. Imagine keeping one seat bone on each side of the horse's spine, if you like. You can guide your horse with your weight so if he wanders off line to the right, you only need to put a bit of weight/sit more heavily on your left seat bone to bring him back, then even up again once he is where you want him. For example, if he is banking in badly to the left in canter, put plenty of weight on your right seat bone and down your right leg and keep your upper body upright. *Do not lean left thinking that you are going with your horse.* This creates a top-heavy, very influential weight aid, which will pull your horse even further left, and could be dangerous.

In the Western sport of barrel racing, rider and horse are almost entirely reliant on weight aids. Here, the rider's weight is to the left, so the horse is turning left and the outside (right) rein is neck-reining the horse to the left, pressing on the side of the neck. These techniques are useful for most active Western sports, in polo and in gymkhana games. Note that this totally relaxed rider's upper body remains quite upright for safety and balance in this extreme sport

TRY THIS TO TURN LEFT

From the seat and legs viewpoint, to turn left all you have to do is put a little weight on your left seat bone and push it forward an inch or so, no more. Do this without tilting your upper body. The aid can be enhanced, if necessary, by dropping some weight down your left leg, on to your stirrup and out through your heel. (Don't let your foot swing forward.) If you do this while your horse is moving, he will turn left. In rising trot, you can push your left seat bone forward a little on the 'forward' phase and apply the weight on the 'sit' phase.

How does it work? The horse feels this weight on the left side of his back and will naturally move underneath it – that is, move left – to balance himself. You have experimented with thinking and looking where you want to go (p.114), so you can combine that technique with the weight aid to excellent effect.

What is your right leg supposed to do? It often does not have to do anything, but you can use it to support your request by putting it back a little from the hip, which, having learned to relax your seat and legs, you will now be quite able to do. If you do what is usually done – bend your outside knee to move only the lower leg back and not the thigh as well, your heel will probably rise and the aid is not so comfortable or supportive to the horse. The whole leg going back a little feels irresistible and easier for the horse to understand because it is unlike any other leg aid you will use.

What happens to the shoulders? The left shoulder goes with the left seat bone – forwards to turn instead of, as is often taught, level or even backwards. Although moving the shoulder may not directly apply weight to the seat, the horse can feel its inclination and putting it back – and the right shoulder forwards – twists the rider's body, which blocks the energy flow through it. This is more uncomfortable than the more logical and comfortable position of having the shoulders above the hips. Discomfort creates tension, even a little, which is not what either the rider or the horse needs.

Make sure your left shoulder is directly above your left hip, forward into the turn. You are thinking positively about where you want to go and are looking there with your eyes (your face directed between your horse's ears), and your right leg is suggesting 'left' by being back from the hip and laid lightly against the horse's side. Again, the horse will be able to feel the backward inclination of your thigh through the saddle. Your right shoulder stays above your right hip – it does *not* move forward.

TURN LEFT, INSIDE AIDS

4. She is looking where she wants to go.

3. She has opened the inside rein a little (carried it away from the horse's neck).

1. The rider is putting her inside seat bone and shoulder forward slightly.

2. She is putting a little weight on her seat bone and down her inside leg to the stirrup. (Remember: where you put your weight your horse will go.)

What about hands and reins? Again, it is simple and logical. Your left rein does not pull the horse round the turn. It may give the lightest tweak if the horse is distracted and looking in the wrong direction but, basically, all you need do is bring your left hand forward and left a little, keeping your elbow bent and at your hip, to invite the horse round the turn.

Slightly open the fingers of your right hand – without moving the hand forward – to give the horse room to bend his neck to the left, and press the rein sideways on his neck just in front of the withers, gently pushing his forehand left. You can also apply this sideways aid with your knuckles or fingertips – the message is the same. Usually one on-off press is enough but you can repeat it, if necessary. The reason this works is because this is the 'go away' message horses give each other naturally. Horses tend to lean into steady pressure but move away from intermittent pressure.

Here's a summary of the aids to turn. It will take you about 60 seconds to read but only one second to do it.

1. Place the inside seat bone slightly forward and maybe put a little weight on it and down the inside leg – without tilting the upper body sideways or collapsing the outside side of the waist. Bring your inside shoulder forward into the turn, too, and look over to where you want to go.

> *'Pressing the rein sideways on the neck mimics the 'go away' message horses give to each other.'*

2. Invite the horse round the turn by bringing the inside hand away from the neck into the turn and slightly forward.

3. Open the fingers of the outside hand to allow the horse to flex around his turn and press the outside rein sideways (not backwards) against the horse's neck just in front of the withers in an on-off movement.

4. Place your outside leg slightly back from the hip, not the knee, and gently lie it sideways down its inside length, against the horse's side. Keep your outside shoulder above it.

5. The only job of the inside leg is to press intermittently sideways just on or behind the girth if the horse's pace needs maintaining. Otherwise just keep it there in position and still.

This simple combination of weight and pressure, plus the powerful influence of the mind and eyes, is quite enough to cause most horses to turn nicely. These same principles apply in all your riding. To repeat, where you look and where you put your weight your horse will go. This applies whether you mean to do it or not! So if your weight is unstable in the saddle, your horse will waver around; if you are still and balanced, your horse will be balanced and his gait will be steady. If you ask your horse to turn right but your weight is over to the left he will probably not turn right well if at all, and may well go left after a fashion.

Refining your seat aids

As you and your horse become more and more used to using the seat for both position and weight aids, and for slowing and stopping, you will find that you can refine your technique even further by simply using your seat to ask for energy and movement and giving other aids. For example, when your horse is used to the inside seat bone being placed forwards for canter he will be quite ready to take up the gait simply from a forward, upward nudge of your inside seat bone in that position, little or no leg being needed. To move off from halt, a little push forward of both seat bones will eventually result in his walking off or making an upward transition to trot. Ultimately, you can work towards obtaining flying changes simply by changing the position of your seat bones during the moment of suspension in canter. Magic!

'Imagine keeping one seat bone on each side of the horse's spine.'

TURN LEFT, OUTSIDE AIDS

5. In this photo, the rider is leaning slightly to the left: it is better to stay upright and apply the weight aids.

4. The outside shoulder does *not* move forward but stays above the outside hip.

3. It is important to use the rein sideways and not backwards. Open your fingers to give with the rein a little and allow the horse to bend around the turn.

1. The rider puts her outside leg back a little from the hip and pushes gently *sideways* with it against the horse's ribs.

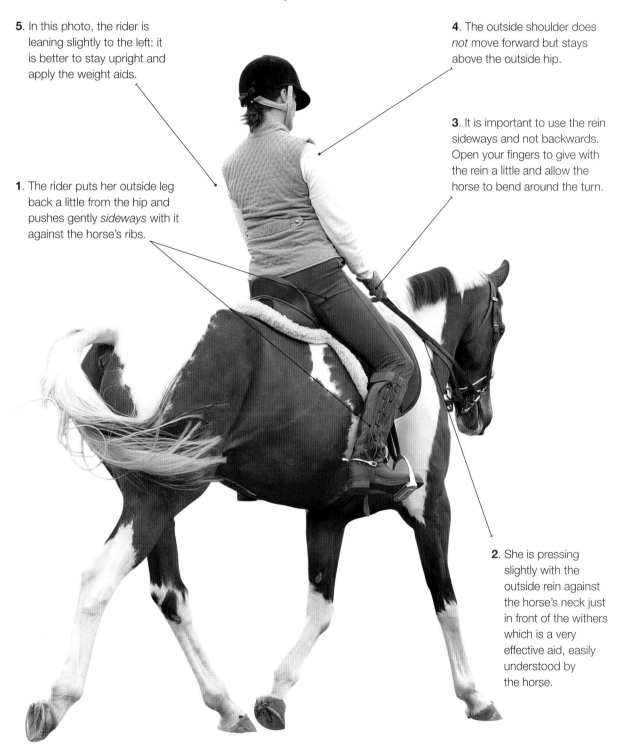

2. She is pressing slightly with the outside rein against the horse's neck just in front of the withers which is a very effective aid, easily understood by the horse.

Rein aids and contact

The rein aids described for turning (on pp.124–127) will have given you a good indication of the principles of this system. The outside rein is often called the Master Rein, being used to control the speed and to direct the horse, the inside one being mainly to communicate little nuances of expression to him, asking him to soften to the bit, to flex in a certain direction and to generally listen. I also use my voice, saying clear, simple words and phrases, and use a horse's name a lot as well, as an attention-getter.

'GIVING' TO THE BIT

Because this is not a schooling manual as such, I shall give here the techniques for asking a horse to give to the bit without going too much into the finer details. With your horse tacked up for work, stand at his head, your back to his tail, and hold his reins, as for riding, under his neck with the reins coming straight back to your hands horizontal to the ground. Let's say that you are standing on his right so your left rein is your outside, Master, rein and your right one your inside one.

Take up the contact – outside rein. Your horse will be standing with his head and neck in his natural position. Take up the contact on the outside (left) rein so that you have a firm but gentle, 'hand-holding' pressure or 'feel' on it. For all that has been said about not pulling on the reins, you do need to let your horse feel a gentle but significant and reassuring contact on the rein and the only way you can presently do that is to close your fingers on the rein so that you feel backwards very slightly. Keep this contact steady but not stiff or rigid, which could hurt the horse or cause him to pull against it.

Take up the contact – inside rein. Pick up your inside (right) rein and apply the same contact but do a 'squeeze-and-release, squeeze-and-release' movement on it by closing and opening your fingers on it. This may involve, again, a slight backward pressure to create the 'ask'. You are asking the horse to open his lower jaw and so give or flex to the pressure of the bit in his mouth. If you do it too lightly at present, the horse may not respond. If you do it too hard he will take exception to it and may resist more

Many horses go happily in bitless bridles – and without saddles

actively. Apply about the same strength as you would when holding a child's hand as you take him across the road. So your squeeze is a slight backward feel that you immediately release. It is not a jab or a yank – it is just a squeeze applying backward pressure with one rein on the jaw to ask him to relax it.

It will only take two or three tries or so to get most horses to soften to the bit in this way. The instant he does, stop asking and keep your hands still (don't bring them backwards) with a very light contact, praising him. The next step is to ask him to do this on the other rein, with your right as the outside rein and the left as the inside one, so that he responds to your request on both reins.

On the move and on board. When the horse has got the idea of softening to the bit with you on the ground and stationary, try this exercise at the walk on both reins, maybe in the yard or school, then mount and repeat the same thing from the saddle, first standing still, then in walk. Once you are moving you need to maintain energy with your legs (see p.132) – a good, swinging walk with your hand-holding contact on the outside rein and your squeeze-and-release on the inside one. You can use the same technique in trot and canter. It may help to have a sensible friend to keep your horse moving or to give the squeeze aid from the ground until the horse gets the idea. Just a few tries per ride will do the trick.

The crucial point – stop the squeeze aid the instant the horse gives because this tells him that he has done what you were asking. Praise him, maintain a light contact and keep walking, trotting or whatever. If he 'comes above the bit' again, pokes his nose, leans on the bit or anything similar, repeat the aid until he gets the idea that he needs to go with a soft jaw and hold himself there in self-balance with a very light contact from you. If he has not done this before but is used to leaning on the bit or being held in, at whatever level he works, he will be using unaccustomed muscles, so do not expect him to hold the posture for more than a few strides per time. If you are sensitive and consistent he will become stronger in the required muscles and soon will readily go in self-balance.

Contact in brief

· Have a hand-holding feel on outside rein
· Use squeeze-and-release on the inside rein – opening and closing your fingers on the rein
· Stop the squeeze the instant the horse 'gives'

To get the horse used to the idea of giving to the bit and softening, use one rein as your outside rein (here the right), keeping it in a still, gentle contact. On the other, give intermittent squeezes and gentle 'feels' to ask the horse to relax his lower jaw and flex at the poll

Ike gets the message and softens to the aid to a point where the front of his face is just in front of the vertical. He relaxes his lower jaw by opening it very slightly and flexes at the poll. Because of his conformation in the throat area, he does not find flexing at the poll easy and is never asked for much flexion, just enough to give a soft feel to the hand

Softening to the bit and contact

One of the main difficulties I find with riders who have not been able to acquire a good equestrian education is how to get a horse to soften to the bit: indeed, many of them do not know why this is desirable. Often they have been told by instructors to 'get his head in' without being told how or why, or to 'get him going forward', without being able to distinguish between 'forward' and 'speed'. Neither of these two instructions is of any use at all in encouraging a horse to go well.

The reason we require a horse to give softly to the bit with a neck which is stretched freely forward and out, with the nose just in front of the vertical is because in the self-balanced state, the back and belly will automatically rise, the hindquarters flex at the croup (the lumbo-sacral joint) and tilt under, and the hind legs reach further under the horse, so that he is going in the required vertebral bow. His muscles will strengthen to hold this posture and he will find working in independent balance easier, provided the rider remains balanced and does nothing to interfere with him. (If you are still unsure what you should be looking for in your horse's way of going and how he should carry himself, reread pp.28–59.)

According to all the best, traditional standards, the object of all equestrianism is to get the horse to go as freely, athletically, willingly, lightly and joyfully as possible under a rider. This means as close as possible to his natural way of going with a little more emphasis on raising the back (remember the 'vertebral bow') because he needs to do this to bear weight safely and relatively effortlessly. Hauling and holding in the horse's head will not achieve this and neither will being 'over-soft' and not asking the horse to take any contact at all (going on 'washing lines').

Riding the headless horse

It is possible to never, or hardly ever, take any contact and, if a rider has no coordination at all, is not capable of keeping her hands still (never mind independent of her body movements), and has little feel for her horse's mouth, using the 'no hands' method of riding, or 'riding the headless horse' is better than hanging on to his mouth and torturing him at every step.

To ride without hands you need to develop communication through your seat and by using your voice: it is possible to ride quite actively this way. However, although your horse will develop his body to enable him to carry weight, he will not develop his musculature in the same way as a horse asked to go in the now-familiar vertebral bow posture. He will tend to have a rather plank-like physique and way of going, not the rounded and all-over strong physique and agility of a horse ridden with the aim of producing self-balance and, ultimately, the goal of all consummate equestrians – self-carriage, in which his balance is as good under his rider as when at liberty in the field.

There are some horses who are never happy with any kind of bit contact, either because they just don't like it or have bad memories from the past. Also, some riders may have naturally insensitive hands and find it difficult to create a 'feeling' contact

With horses who dislike or are afraid of any bit contact, or riders who are not able to develop a sensitive contact, the technique of 'riding the headless horse', that means using little or no rein contact, can be a good solution

This horse is cantering in a good posture, freely and easily, clearly in self-balance as his rider gives the inside rein

'When he is in self-carriage, the horse responds to the lightest of weight and pressure aids and has no need to resist because he is not unbalanced or unhappy.'

Mouths and bits

If your horse is in the habit of resisting in his mouth, first get his teeth and mouth checked and if he still seems particularly resistant try differently acting bits. I do not like single-jointed snaffles because they do not mould to the shape of the horse's mouth, have quite a nasty squeezing action and can press into the roof of the mouth. I prefer French-link snaffles or any with a comfortable lozenge, which makes the bit into a more rounded, rather than V, shape in the mouth. The point is to find a bit which the horse both respects and is comfortable in.

Pelhams

Many horses that, for various reasons, are heavy and insensitive or resisting in snaffles (assuming that the rider does not have harsh hands) go very kindly in pelham bits, becoming much lighter in the hand and more attentive and responsive. Although, sadly, they are not 'legal' for most dressage competitions, pelhams are widely used in other disciplines.

It has been said that they are 'downward' bits, presumably meaning that they encourage horses to overbend and go behind the bit. This is only so if the rider uses too much curb pressure. When they are used correctly, not with roundings but with two pairs of reins, the curb is held looser than the bridoon and used only when a little

more response is needed, then released. This is not possible, of course, when roundings are used: they unavoidably create too much curb pressure.

The balance of the pelham means that just putting it in the horse's mouth creates a very slight curb effect, which alone is often sufficient to improve the horse's head-carriage and relax his mouth. Horses that fuss, lean or resist in a snaffle often settle and lighten up quickly in a pelham. Correctly fitted and adjusted, a smooth, mullen-mouthed/half-moon pelham is the answer for many horses. (For more information on bits and tack in general, see pp.60–63.)

Driving horses

Some horses present problems when ridden if they have been badly driven previously. The practice of many drivers to hang on to the mouth, often injuring it and not educating the horse's responses to the bit, and also to not train the horse adequately to the voice before putting him to a vehicle, causes untold distress for the horses, and problems for their future riders. Even if the horse is taken right back to scratch and reschooled from the ground onwards, it can be a wise idea to use a bit with a different action and feel from the one he was driven in, so that there is no mental connection between the two and he is less likely to continue with his previous unwanted reactions to the bit.

Leg aids

The leg aids are your main means of getting your horse to move. With your seat loose and moulded around your horse, and the legs draped lightly down around his sides, it is easier to give effective, correct leg aids. Have your stirrups at a comfortable length so that you can stretch your legs down but not so long that you are 'tiptoeing' in trot and keep losing them. As your seat deepens you will find that you gradually need them longer but your ambition should be to be comfortable, balanced and effective, not solely to have long stirrups!

The legs can be used in the position the rider needs to control the horse's movements, but at all times try to give your aids with a downward leg and with the insides of your calves. Putting the leg forward on the girth is helpful for turning or controlling the forehand, having it just behind the girth is for most riding, and using it back from the hip behind the girth instructs or controls the hindquarters

The correct, basic seat is the same for halt, walk, sitting trot and also for canter other than at fast paces. This is an excellent position at walk. It would be easy to draw a vertical line from the rider's ear, down through her shoulder, hip and heel

USING YOUR LEGS

To give a basic 'please go forward' or 'produce more energy' aid, simply give a quick inward pinch, on-and-off, with the insides of your calves. Note the word 'inward'. This means exactly that – not upward or backward. So often we see lower legs brought back, heels raised, toes down and the heels ground into the horse's sides, and kept pressed on until he moves, in a very crude aid, which will never make for subtlety or lightness and which puts the rider out of balance and into a perched position.

Asking for halt-walk and walk-trot. Think 'inward squeeze' or 'inward pinch' and do exactly that – on-off – and maybe give a vocal command as well. Don't forget to release with your fingers to 'open the door'. If you get no response, try again a little firmer with voice and leg, and if a third request is necessary, back it up with a tap or light flick with a schooling whip just behind your leg. With the sort of horse we are, hopefully, using for learning this new technique (cooperative and reasonably well-schooled) the third attempt will probably not be necessary.

Getting canter. For canter, from either walk or sitting trot, warn your horse that you are going to ask for canter by putting your inside seat bone and shoulder forward a little for two or three strides, then give your aid. For example, if you wish to canter right, push your right seat bone and shoulder forward a little, your left leg down back from the hip and try to time your aid so that you squeeze with it as the outside hind (which starts the stride) is about to leave the ground. Earlier, you practised feeling which hind leg is moving forward from the feel under your seat (pp.80–90) and this is where you put it to practical use. If you cannot manage this, don't worry; just position yourself

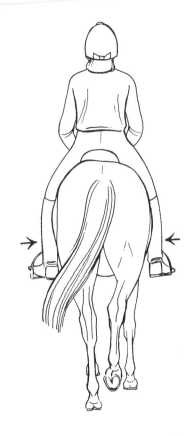

Get into the habit of using your legs in an *inward* quick squeeze or pinch, rather than kicking back with the heels

as described and give a quick squeeze with your outside leg. Most horses will take off to that aid. If you need to squeeze with your inside (right) leg, too, do so.

Throughout the canter, keep your inside seat bone and shoulder forward a little. This 'position aid' is your horse's instruction to stay in canter. Of course, absorb the movement as described earlier, as well. With practise and relaxation, this is not difficult. If you are stiff and tense, it is.

The same basic position can be seen here in sitting trot. There is no nodding of the head (a very common fault) in a good sitting trot, all the movement being absorbed in the lower back and seat with the upper body being held upright but not rigid and stiff

133

Returning to trot. To come back to trot, all you need to do is return the seat bone and shoulder level with the outside ones, and your horse will trot. There is no need for any rein aid. The horse trots because your seat is no longer positioned in harmony with his own back position for canter, so he is less comfortable and he prefers to trot. If you have been having trouble maintaining canter, or getting it in the first place, you should find that using this position aid largely solves the problem, particularly if you do not hang on to the inside rein, which puts off many horses from cantering freely.

This seat and leg position is applicable for canter whether your horse is cantering on a straight line or on a bend or circle. In walk and trot, your shoulders and seat bones are positioned exactly along the radius of the circle, each turn or bend being part of a circle (see diagram, p.95).

> *'To come back to trot, all you need to do is return the inside seat bone and shoulder level with the outside ones, and your horse will trot.'*

Again, here in canter, the upper body is held upright and not allowed to rock backwards and forwards during the stride. Often, as the first hind foot of the stride hits the ground and the forehand rises, the tendency is to allow the upper body to swing forwards. When the leading leg lands and the hindquarters rise, the upper body is inclined to swing backwards

Legs in brief

Give leg aids with a downward leg and with the insides of your calves, and have the leg just behind the girth for most riding

Put the leg forward on the girth for turning or controlling the forehand

Move the leg back – from the hip – to behind the girth to instruct or control the hindquarters

Putting the leg back in this way is not so effective and tends to collapse the rider at the hip

Transitions

Once you have the basics of the seat, rein and leg aids, transitions become much easier and more elegant for the pair of you.

UPWARD TRANSITIONS

For halt to walk and walk to trot, use the legs in an on-off pinch, aiming to get a response from lighter and lighter aids over time. It is very important to open your fingers a little on the reins to allow the horse to move forward and not inadvertently prevent him doing so. The trot to canter transition is described on p.133 and p.138, the gait being maintained by means of your seat and shoulder position, forward with the leading side of the back.

If you want to lengthen the horse's stride within a gait or move from collected to medium, or medium to extended paces, simply use the legs as described and make sure you remember to open the fingers a little to allow the horse to move forward and onward. This releasing with the fingers also encourages expression and swing in the gait.

Remember to breathe! An exaggerated outward breath, with some energy in time with the leg aid, helps an upward transition.

HALT TO WALK

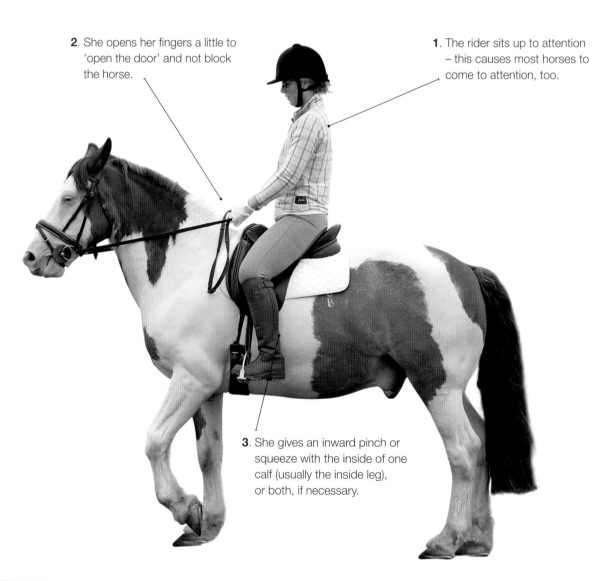

2. She opens her fingers a little to 'open the door' and not block the horse.

1. The rider sits up to attention – this causes most horses to come to attention, too.

3. She gives an inward pinch or squeeze with the inside of one calf (usually the inside leg), or both, if necessary.

WALK TO TROT

Alexa and Ike are walking along actively and freely

Alexa opens her fingers, then squeezes with her calves in an on-off movement

Ike springs up into trot, adopting the trot's diagonal form. Alexa drops her legs and starts a neat rising trot, keeping a light contact on the bit so as not to block Ike's transition

Ike gives her a lively, free trot, Alexa keeps her legs long, toned and still so there is no flapping or swinging about

Ike continues to trot along happily

TROT TO CANTER

1. Alexa brings her inside seat bone forward a little to warn Ike that canter is coming.

3. She puts her outside leg back from the hip, not just the knee, and gives Ike a nudge with it.

2. She opens her fingers to give him the necessary freedom to change gait.

Ike has brought his outside hind forward and lifted up and off into canter. He has a bouncy canter gait and Alexa, always keeping her inside seat bone forward, is also forward a little in the saddle to help her to go with the transition as Ike takes off

Cantering along, Alexa has her inside seat bone forward and keeps her legs relaxed and down and her upper body upright

DOWNWARD TRANSITIONS

Downward transitions often turn into a pulling match, which is unpleasant for horse, rider and onlooker and can spoil a horse's mouth and his reactions to rein aids in general. The transition can be from one gait to another or within a gait, say to shorten the stride or change from extension to medium, or down to working paces or collection, according to the level at which you are working.

From canter to trot, simply bring your inside (leading) seat bone and shoulder back level with the outside ones and your horse will trot. A noticeable inward breath will also have a slowing, downward effect. Also, just raise your chest a little and stretch up a bit more as these 'arresting' movements also help the transition.

CANTER TO TROT

3. Gently squeeze or resist intermittently with the hands (no pulling).

2. This is enough to signal to most horses to resume trot. Another aid for slowing or halting, easily recognized by horses, is to slightly tighten the muscles of your tummy, back and buttocks.

1. To come down from canter to trot, Alexa brings back her inside seat bone level with the outside one.

To go from trot to walk and walk to halt, try the following aids, which are gentle, clear, and logical because the horse responds to them naturally.

If you are doing rising trot, start by gradually slowing your forward-sit movement so that you are slightly behind the rhythm of your horse. Also, think, and perhaps say, 'walk' to him and, without pulling on the reins, keep your hands gently still and just tighten your fingers. Breathe in and sense when he is about to walk, then sit in the saddle normally. If you merely want a shortening of stride, use the slower forward-sit but tighten your fingers and simply relax them again as he reaches the length of stride you want.

If in sitting trot, again slow your rhythm slightly in the saddle as you absorb his movements, tighten your fingers on the reins and keep your hands still, stretch your body up a little more and breathe in, until the horse reaches the way of going you require. If you want to walk, think and say 'walk' to him and tense your seat muscles. Then use your normal walk movements and rein contact. Many horses need a little nudge with the inside leg to keep them walking on with energy after coming down from trot.

To go from walk to halt, the procedure is similar. Stop moving your seat with your horse's movements and tighten the muscles of your buttocks and thighs. This will

TROT TO WALK

Ike goes smoothly from canter into the diagonal trot action while Alexa remains balanced and non-interfering

Ike has flexed at the poll nicely here and the pair is moving actively along in sitting trot

WALK TO HALT

Anne and Lucy are walking along in an active walk

Anne tenses her tummy, back and buttocks and resists gently the movement of Lucy's head in walk

raise you slightly in the saddle which, I feel, is better than sitting down heavily, as many riders do, as this encourages the horse to flatten his back and makes it difficult for him to bring his hind legs under in a gathered, balanced halt. Rising up in the saddle, not consciously but because your muscles are a little tensed, enables your horse to raise his back and bring his hindquarters and legs under. Stop moving your fingers with his head movements and slightly tighten your fingers on the reins. If, possibly out of habit, he pulls against the reins and resists, just lightly squeeze each one alternately to ask him to give and to make the bit unsteady in his mouth so that he has nothing to lean on.

Never, ever keep up a constant, steady pull with a horse who is resisting the halt aid as it will just make him worse and confirm the old adage 'it takes two to pull'. Also, do not rock from side to side with the horse's action as you tighten the muscles of your seat and thighs to stop. Do not tense them so much that you become stiff and rigid. It is just a slight tensing and stopping of absorption of his movement, which will naturally tell him that walk is no longer required and he should stop.

To come down to walk, Alexa tenses the muscles of her tummy, back and seat and resists gently with her hands ...

... and on the very next diagonal, Ike obliges with a lovely, soft downward transition to walk

On the next step, Lucy halts. Anne remains upright and relaxes her aids

HALT TO REIN-BACK

The transition from halt to rein-back is again one that causes a lot of trouble. You should not, and cannot, pull the horse backwards with the reins. If you pull on the mouth, the horse's head is pulled in and he experiences severe discomfort in his mouth. Instead, lift your seat slightly so that he can lift his back and hindquarters to step backwards. Keep a steady, light but definite contact on the bit and brush backwards with the insides of your calves, saying 'back'. The bit contact tells him that you do not want him to go forward and the backward direction of the legs suggests that he goes in that direction. Also, he should be familiar with the command 'back' from handling on the ground. A friend gently pushing on his chest or lightly tapping it with a whip will help him get the idea.

REIN-BACK

Poor Ike! But Alexa is not being rough with him. They demonstrate how not to ask for rein-back. Leaning back weights the hindquarters and makes it difficult for the horse to step backwards. Although the rider's legs need to go back, this position not only looks awful but also puts Alexa even more out of balance. Raising the hands and pulling back in desperation are both very common and neither works. Like the little soldier he is, Ike (who can do a perfectly good rein-back) raises his head, flattens his back and tries, with difficulty, to oblige

Aids in conclusion

I hope that you agree that the aids given here are logical and easily understood by the horse because they are based on his natural way of working, also that they are humane, supportive and effective. In the final chapter, I go through an imaginary schooling session and a ride and think through most of the techniques described to see how they work in practice.

Anne and Lucy demonstrate good aids for a rein-back. Anne has lightened her seat by leaning forward slightly from the hips, has a passively resisting contact on the reins to tell Lucy not to walk forward and is brushing backward with her legs. Lucy is reining back correctly, her legs moving in diagonal pairs

9

Putting it all together

By the time you have got here, you might be feeling encouraged to start putting everything you have read into practice – if you haven't tried some of it already. On the other hand, your mind might be reeling with all the new ideas and techniques. The aim of this chapter is to help you to imagine yourself on a horse – in a manège, out riding or at a competition – and riding using these concepts.

Let's begin

Absorb the theory first and do some dismounted work on your own such as the limbering up exercises, yoga, meditation or whatever you are drawn to. Also start thinking to your horse and using the visualizations because these always help.

Next practise the posture, the loose seat and feeling the horse's movements, and adapting your seat and legs to them. Then start putting the seat, rein and leg aids into practice, beginning at the walk, then the trot and canter and maybe the gallop, and, if you want to jump, try the seat I have recommended over low obstacles.

Don't make the mistake of thinking that this way of riding is only for the manège. This is an entire, effective and kind way to ride under any circumstances and in any discipline – so here we go. As you read on, you may have a giggle and think that what I describe isn't going to happen, but believe me these principles really do work. My intention is to give you the idea of how to apply them, mind control permitting, out riding. When they become second nature, you will find that you are a much more powerful rider without being forceful. We all have emergencies when our instincts take over, but – well, read on and put yourself in the picture.

'A word of warning: don't try to do too much at once and then blame yourself when you make mistakes. This does not make for a calm, positive mind!'

Imagine this

You've done a few loosening-up exercises and taken care to tack up your horse comfortably. Perhaps you decide to warm him up on the ground first, especially if he has been stabled and so not moving around much. This will give his tissues a chance to loosen and warm up without the stress of carrying weight. Loose work, in my view, should not come first because the horse might perform all sorts of high jinks, which will strain unprepared muscles: leading around or gentle, controlled lungeing on very large circles, ovals and straight lines seems more logical, with the horse unconstrained by training aids – just wearing a cavesson or bridle. At this stage, it is important that he has freedom of his head and neck to fully stretch them, which will affect the whole of his body.

When you mount, you do so from a mounting block so as to save his back and your saddle, and manage to get into the saddle without putting a foot in the stirrup. You completely relax your seat and legs and allow them to drape and mould loosely around your horse. Depending on circumstances and your horse's temperament, you might decide not to take up your stirrups yet but to give yourself a little time to adopt your riding posture and also to sink lightly into your position in and around the saddle. If your horse is likely to play around, of course, or if you are in an exciting environment for him, you'll prefer to take your stirrups and also keep a reasonable contact until he settles, for safety reasons.

You ask him to walk off with a single light, inward pinch with the insides of your calves and opening your fingers. This doesn't work, so you repeat it a little stronger adding a verbal request and your horse walks off. As soon as possible, you give him a completely free rein and encourage him to stretch and swing along, keeping your seat loose and working on sensing his back and hind leg movements. You come to a corner and, rather than letting him take you around it, you turn just before it by putting your inside seat bone and shoulder forward a little and maybe pressing sideways against him with your outside leg and rein, or just giving him a light push with the knuckles of your outside hand, looking round the corner.

Bring your horse in on to the inside track by weighting your inside seat bone a little. Here he cannot psychologically lean on the fence and both of you have to make use of your outside aids. You do a few circuits (no more than one on each rein) in walk, changing rein frequently by means of your seat and eyes. Then you give another inward squeeze with your calves and go up into rising trot – forward, sit, forward, sit (rather than up and down) – keeping your rein loose, again changing direction often. It is important that you keep your horse in horizontal balance to save his forelegs and encourage him to keep his own body under control.

You decide he and you are ready to canter on your loose rein. You calmly and gently adopt sitting trot and warn him of your intention by putting your inside seat bone and shoulder slightly forward. To ask him for canter, you put your outside leg back from the hip and give an inward nudge with it, ideally when the outside hind is about to lift off. Your horse misses the transition so you don't try again immediately but restore a rhythmic, balanced and calm sitting trot. You emphasize your inside seat bone forward and give the aid again using both legs, remembering to picture canter to your horse and giving the vocal word as well. This time he takes off in a smooth transition. Again, it is important to keep him in horizontal balance.

As you canter, you keep your seat aligned with his back – so your inside side is forward a little – and keep your upper body upright, taking up the movement with your lower back and hips. You find that he is coming in off your track and looking to the outside. To correct this, you put some weight on your outside seat bone and down your outside leg which is slightly back from the hip although not so far as when you gave the aid for canter. (Where you put your weight your horse will go, remember.) You also keep your inside leg in place down the girth and maybe give intermittent inward pushes with the whole leg to encourage him to take his weight out. Little vibrations down the inside rein ask him to look in around the track. You allow him to swing along and loosen up, then come back to trot by moving your inside seat bone and shoulder back until they are level with the outside ones.

You warm up like this on both reins for a few minutes, then come down to walk then halt for a rest. You decide to stay in the school for a little while and walk off again, taking up a comfortable, hand-holding contact and, with little squeezes down your inside rein, ask your horse to flex to the bit. This gentle relaxation of the poll and jaw and his neck stretching forward and down encourages him to lift his belly and back and tilt his hindquarters under, so his hind legs reach forward. You work in this posture for a minute or so, maintaining 'thrust' with your leg aids, then rest before working similarly on the other rein. Use your seat and outside aids to change rein.

You repeat this work in walk, trot and canter, telling yourself at all times to think with your seat, to use your seat and leg aids primarily and to be very ready to sense when your horse needs a break. Keeping horses 'in outline' for many minutes at a time is stressful to them and not good for muscle health.

'Frequent breaks encourage circulation through loose tissues and so enhance muscle health.'

When you have worked like this for about half an hour, you decide to go out for a ride around. On the hack, you come across some household rubbish that someone has fly-tipped on the path, which your horse does not like at all! There is a bright, white object (an old stove) in a place where there is normally nothing but juicy, aromatic grass and brambles! There are also some walkers on the path with children and dogs so a horse prancing about is not only unsafe but also bad for equestrian public relations. You give your horse a halt aid some metres from the object – squeezing your seat and thighs and gently stopping the movement of your hands, resuming controlled relaxation in halt. He stands, a bit on edge but still. The walkers pass and you want to go ahead but, even though he has had chance to look at the rubbish from a distance he still does not want to pass it.

Just as you are approaching it to let him examine it more closely, a bird flies up from behind it, squawking. That does it! Your horse whips round preparing to head for home but you keep your presence of mind! You give your normal halt aid – tense your seat and thighs and stop moving your hands – and add a couple of persuasive refinements: you bring your upper body back a little and turn your wrists so that your fingernails are to the sky, as well as using whatever vocal commands he understands for 'slow down' and 'stop'. This has the effect of bringing his forehand up towards you and his weight back on to his hindquarters and of slowing him. You restore equilibrium, thankfully, then turn him back to the object of his fear with a firm seat and leg aid (inside side of your body forward into the turn and weight on the seat bone) and push on the outside of his body with your fist and leg. He comes round but back pedals a bit without actually napping.

You are determined to pass the old stove because he has recently started shying occasionally and you don't want a habit to start. You resist the temptation to hunch forward, flap your arms and legs and kick on because, in the past, this has only resulted in your horse going firmly backwards. So you put your horse into position for shoulder-in curving away from the stove. Your outside aids (nearest the stove) bend him on a curve away from it: your outside leg is back and down his side, controlling the hindquarters, and your outside rein is pushing his head and neck away, supported by your inside rein asking for flexion that way. Your outside hip is forward, pointing up the track – where you are looking calmly, firmly and positively – and you weight that seat bone. Your inside leg strongly acts with intermittent pressure just behind the girth and your voice is telling him calmly but unmistakably to 'walk on'. Your horse feels that you are in control, and although he is not yet calm he does go. You praise him and continue past it.

Once past, you straighten up by bringing your outside seat bone back and stopping asking for flexion with your inside rein. You naturally want to praise your horse, and yourself, again, and can chalk up a notable success.

You arrive at a spot where there are some fallen tree trunks, inviting a bit of fun jumping. You tackle a low one first from trot. You assume your rising trot position, upper body angled a little forward from the hips, not the waist, with your back flat, your shoulders back and down and your chest up. Your legs are dropped down round your horse with your lower legs and upper arms held vertically downwards – and you are in terrific balance. You have a gentle but reassuring feel on your horse's mouth and he knows you are with him. You squeeze him on in a working trot and fold down as he rises under you to pop over it. Your hands follow down towards his mouth.

> *'Your legs are dropped down round your horse with your lower legs and upper arms held vertically downwards – and you are in terrific balance.'*

There is another, slightly higher trunk ahead to your left so you put the left side of your body forward and look there, sending your horse round with sideways pressure from your outside rein and leg. Your horse spots the trunk and decides to canter, actually left canter like the sensible boy he is. No big deal – you go with him, securely balanced in your position so that you have no need to pull yourself up with the reins. You fold down from your hip and knee joints, with your breastbone down towards his withers and your hands following his mouth downwards as he rounds beautifully over it. On landing, you stay in your slightly forward position while he gets away.

You get a perfect jump and landing but your horse is so exhilarated that he decides to have a buck on the other side. You tell him 'no' or whatever he understands for a reprimand, sit up and use your legs to get forward movement. You also raise your hands *upwards, not backwards*, with intermittent pressure on the bit to get his head up, and he stops bucking. Well done! But you don't want that to become the norm. You take the jump again and this time he just canters away on the other side of it, while you praise him.

There is another tree trunk that you have always wanted to try a little further on. It is in a good, clear spot and the ground is fine – it's just a little bigger than those you have tackled before, but he seems to be going so well that you decide to go for it. You canter around establishing

your position, balance and rhythm and calmly and firmly place him towards it. Your best plan is to determine the speed and direction and let the horse see his own stride. You ride confidently forward, and do *not* throw everything to the wind in your approach. Your horse is definitely up for it so, provided you don't interfere with him, you'll both arrive safely on the other side, with another success to chalk up.

You canter freely but calmly towards the tree trunk, buoyed up by your recent successes, and keep your contact light but there. Your horse checks slightly as he balances himself, you squeeze with your legs and keep your hands independent, he takes off, you follow his movement by folding right down, and retain your secure balance by keeping your lower legs vertically down. Because you are in such good balance and your horse can, therefore, carry you over in freedom, you do not need your hands to keep yourself in position or in the saddle. You are able to let your horse's mouth draw your hands down with it in a straight line, giving his head and neck, and therefore his whole body, every chance to reach out and over the jump in a smooth arc.

You're over! What a thrill that was! Your horse lands and you stay up out of the saddle a little and allow your

ankle joints, in particular, to absorb the impact of landing. Your hands stay down but in touch and give your horse the freedom to regain his balance, which he does quickly and gets away. You can hardly believe it but you've finally jumped 'the big one'. You don't push your luck by doing it again but rest on your laurels, stroke him and carry on home.

'Because you are in such good balance and your horse can, therefore, carry you over in freedom, you do not need your hands to keep yourself in position or in the saddle.'

You walk the last mile home on a long rein to bring your horse in cool and let his muscles stretch out naturally after his efforts. Your inner glow sets you up for the rest of the day and you have every right to be pleased with both of you. Hopefully, your horse can relax in the field with his friends and you can indulge in whatever you most enjoy – although you may just have done that.

Further information and suggested reading

The Classical Riding Club

The principles and techniques recommended in this book, including the techniques described for jumping, are entirely based on the codes and methods of the various classical schools of riding, particularly the Portuguese and old French schools. In addition, they are founded on the ongoing sciences of equine biodynamics and psychology and also very much take into account modern welfare aspects of riding and training horses.

The Classical Riding Club is an on-line organization for people who want to ride in a more logical and kinder way and are interested in the proven methods of the various classical schools. The club produces an on-line, downloadable, quarterly newsletter full of helpful and thought-provoking articles, information on events, book reviews and excerpts from the Masters old and new, plus other features. The club also has a Trainers' Directory listing trainers in various parts of the world, although mainly in the UK, the club being based in Scotland.

In the suggested reading list (right), you will see a book by Sylvia Loch. Sylvia is a classical rider, teacher, trainer, author and lecturer, and the founder of The Classical Riding Club.

For more information about it, visit its website at www.classicalriding.co.uk or write to the CRC at Eden Hall, Kelso, Roxburghshire, TD5 7QS, email: crc@classicalriding.co.uk

Suggested reading

Some of these books are in print and some are not. Using the search facilities of the internet and/or a good bookshop offering a search service, you should be able to trace most of them, old or new.

Clayton, Hilary M. *The Dynamic Horse: a biomechanical guide to equine movement and performance* (Sport Horse Publications, Michigan) believed 2005

Lijsen, H.J. and Stanier, Sylvia, *Classical Circus Equitation* (J.A. Allen) 1993

Loch, Sylvia, *Invisible Riding* (Horse's Mouth Publications, D.J. Murphy (Publishers) Ltd.) 2003

McBane, Susan, *100 Ways To Improve Your Riding* (David & Charles) 2004

McBane, Susan, *100 Ways To Improve Your Horse's Schooling* (David & Charles) 2006

McGreevy, Paul, *Equine Behavior: a guide for veterinarians and equine scientists* (Saunders) 2004

McLean, Andrew, *The Truth About Horses* (David & Charles) 2003

Moffett, Heather, *Enlightened Equitation* (David & Charles) 1999

Oliveira, Nuño, any books by this author

Paillard, Jean Saint-Fort, *Understanding Equitation* (Pitman) 1975

Racinet, Jean-Claude, *Another Horsemanship: a manual of riding in the French classical tradition* (Xenophon Press) 1991 and 1994

Rolfe, Jenny, *Ride From The Heart: the art of communication between horse and rider* (J.A. Allen) 2007

Swift, Sally, *Centered Riding* (J.A. Allen) 2006

Swift, Sally, *Centred Riding 2: Further Exploration* (J.A. Allen) 2002

Toptani, Count Ilias, *Modern Show Jumping* (Stanley Paul) 1954 and 1959

Wilson, Anne, *Top Training Methods Explored* (David & Charles) 2004

There are many more good books on riding in a light, effective and humane way. This is just a personal selection to start you off.

Acknowledgments

My sincere thanks go to everyone, human and equine, who gave of their time and patience to stage the photographs for this book and especially to Sally and David Waters of Horsepix for their unfailing professionalism and good humour under stress! The editorial and design teams at David & Charles, as usual, have come up trumps with a book which is visually appealing and easy to 'digest', so helping greatly to get the message through to readers and, ultimately, helping their horses. My particular thanks go to Jo Weeks for being such a patient, sensitive and eagle-eyed copy editor, who has performed above and beyond the call of duty in the pursuit of accuracy and correct impressions. I could not have produced this book without any of you. Thank you so much.

I should like to thank most sincerely all the horses and riders who gave their time so freely and patiently to set up the photographs, especially (in Great Britain) Pauline and Jo with Sky, Anne with Lucy, Alice with Brodie and Alexa with Ike, and (in the USA) Petra with Diamunde and Isabeau, Jacqui with Benson and Sheri with Quint and Phantastique.

Thanks and admiration also to Chief, owned by Caroline Lacey Freeman, for demonstrating his free jumping abilities so enthusiastically.

Jo Birkbeck, BHSII, Holme, north Lancashire can be contacted on 01524 782515.

Index